THE WESTON, CLEVEDON & PORTISHEAD LIGHT RAILWAY

by
Colin G. Maggs

THE OAKWOOD PRESS

© Oakwood Press 1990

ISBN 0 85361 388 5

First published 1964
Second Enlarged Edition 1990
Typeset by Gem Publishing Company, Brightwell, Wallingford, Oxfordshire.

Printed by Alpha Print, Witney, Oxon.

An appropriate comic postcard, where the artist has let his imagination run riot.
Author's Collection

Published by
The OAKWOOD PRESS
P.O.Box 122, Headington, Oxford.

Contents

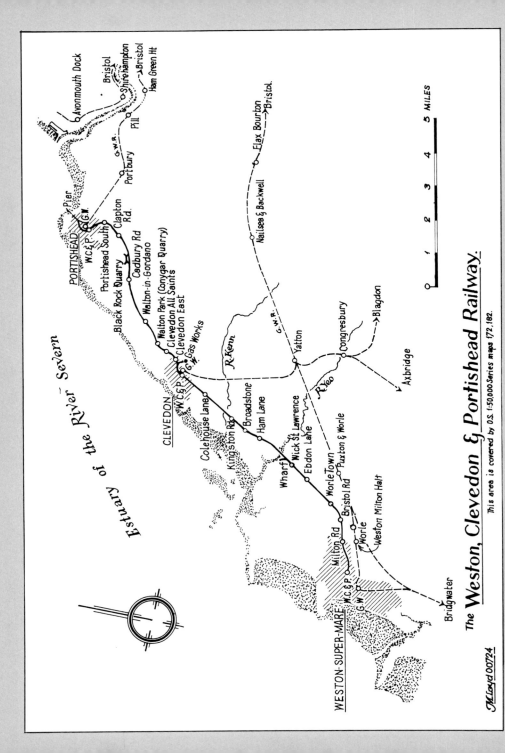

The Weston, Clevedon & Portishead Railway.

This area is covered by O.S. 1:50,000 Series maps 172, 182.

Estuary of the River Severn

Avonmouth Dock

Bristol
Shirehampton
→Bristol
Ham Green Ht
Pill
Portbury
G.W.R.

Pier
PORTISHEAD
W.C.&P.
G.W.
Clapton Rd.
Cadbury Rd
Portishead South
Black Rock Quarry
Walton-in-Gordano
Walton Park (Conygar Quarry)
Clevedon All Saints
Clevedon East
CLEVEDON
W.C.&P.
G.W. Gas Works
Colehouse Lane
Kingston Rd
Broadstone
Ham Lane
Wharf
Wick St. Lawrence
Ebdon Lane
Worle Town
Puxton & Worle
Bristol Rd
Milton Rd
Worle
Weston Milton Halt
WESTON-SUPER-MARE
W.C.&P.
G.W.
Bridgwater

Nailsea & Backwell
Flax Bourton
→Bristol.
G.W.R.
R. Kenn
Yatton
R. Yeo
Congresbury
→Blagdon
Axbridge

0 1 2 3 4 5 MILES

JBLloyd 00724

Chapter One

Early Days

When Parliament passed the Great Western Railway Act on 31st August, 1835, it was quite obvious that, before long, someone would be seeking powers to extend the railway beyond Bristol to Exeter.

A direct line from Bristol to Exeter would have cut straight through the Mendip Hills; Brunel, the Bristol & Exeter Railway's Engineer, realised the importance of avoiding gradients as far as possible, so the only suitable route was to go south-west from Bristol through Yatton and around Bleadon Hill at the western end of the Mendips.

The line passed quite near Portishead, Clevedon and Weston-super-Mare, but a diversion to bring the railway to these towns was thought more trouble than it was worth. Their respective populations in 1831 were 800, 1147 and 1310 but none of these places had yet developed into a holiday resort. Clevedon and Weston could easily have been on the main GWR line had it been considered desirable, but the cost of taking a main line through the Avon Gorge to Portishead would have been a great deterrent.

It was Brunel's policy for places even quite a short distance from the main line to be served by branches, rather than diverting the main line. Examples are the Wallingford and Faringdon branches of the GWR and the Devizes, Bradford-upon-Avon and Frome branches of the Wilts, Somerset & Weymouth Railway.

A single track branch ran to Weston-super-Mare, one and a half miles from Weston Junction, and was opened on 14th June, 1841, the same day as the main line. Branch trains were drawn by horses, passenger trains usually consisting of three four-wheeled unroofed coaches with hard toastrack seats,

The Walker Bros of Wigan locomotive *Clevedon* (with driver George Hancock), seen here in 1898 at Clevedon. Note the 'WCPT' on the buffer beam. It is running as a 2–4–0T so as to be able to negotiate the tight curve to the GWR exchange siding. The low platform and flat-bottomed track can clearly be seen. This engine only saw service for about six months before being replaced by the ex-Furness Railway single wheeler.   *P. Strange Collection*

The Stephenson-built locomotive *Portishead*, again with the distinctive 'WCPT' on the buffer beam, seen here on a train in 1899. The flimsy fence and space between the fence and ballast is very noticeable in this 'posed' photograph.

Courtesy Locomotive Magazine

drawn by three horses in tandem fashion ridden by boys. From the beginning of 1848 a steam hauled express was worked from Weston-super-Mare to Bristol in the morning, with a corresponding down train in the evening. The Weston loop, giving direct through running to and from the West, was not opened until 1st March, 1884.

Meanwhile, on 28th July, 1847 a single track branch 3½ miles in length was opened between the main line at Yatton and Clevedon, a growing watering place, but Portishead at this period was only served by a horse bus to and from Bristol.

With the increase in size of shipping, difficulties were being experienced in getting the larger vessels up the River Avon to Bristol. In order that trade would not be lost from the district, the Bristol & Portishead Pier & Railway was formed on 29th June, 1863 to build a single broad gauge line from Bedminster, Bristol. The line opened on 18th April, 1867 and was worked by the Bristol & Exeter Railway. The associated dock was opened on 30th April, 1879. The railway (but not the dock) was vested in the GWR by an Act of 14th August, 1884.

There was now communication to Weston, Clevedon and Portishead, but no direct link between three growing towns only 8 and 5 miles apart, though a horse bus did run between Clevedon and Portishead. Until the coming of the M5 motorway, there was no direct road between Clevedon and Weston as the River Yeo was not bridged below Congresbury, since there are no villages of consequence *en route*, and the road pattern runs at right angles to the coast rather than parallel. Even now the M5 hardly gives a direct route from Clevedon to Weston.

Chapter Two

The Weston, Clevedon & Portishead Tramway Company

In 1865, while the Bristol & Portishead Railway was under construction, its Engineer, Francis Croughton Stileman, planned a link line from Portishead to the B&E at Clevedon, the route being similar to that eventually constructed. Had the project not proved abortive (plans foundering on a Parliamentary technicality) it would have been worked by the B&E. The Chairman of the Bristol & Portishead Railway, namely Alderman James Ford of Messrs Ford & Canning, (warehousemen) was also a member of the Bristol Dock Board, Director of the Clifton Suspension Bridge Company and the Taff Vale Railway. His son, A. H. Ford, became a Director of the Weston, Clevedon & Portishead Tramway.

In 1880 a Weston-super-Mare resident, James Collings, proposed building a coastal road from Weston to Clevedon at an estimated cost of £3000. A 60 ft long bridge was to cross the River Yeo at Kingston Seymour and the road was to be flanked by trees throughout its entire length.

A preliminary meeting of the promoters of the Weston-super-Mare, Clevedon & Portishead Tramways was held at the Talbot Hotel, Bristol on 11th December, 1884 presided over by W. J. Braikenridge. The Engineers explained how cheaply a tram line could be worked as compared with an ordinary railway, and the great advantage in being able to pick up and put down at any point along the line; also the avoidance of the station ticket nuisance, for it was anticipated that a conductor would pass through a train from end to end collecting fares. They planned for goods to be conveyed only between 8 pm and 8 am in order not to detain passenger traffic. A resolution in favour of the scheme was passed at the meeting and a committee appointed to petition Parliament to accept the Bill.

On 20th December, 1884 the Weston-super-Mare, Clevedon & Portishead Tramways Bill was deposited, J. F. R. Daniel, Secretary to the Bristol & Portishead Railway being the power behind the scheme. Parliamentary expenses, till the passing of the Act on 6th August, 1885, 48 & 49 Vic. cap. 182, were £3858. 5s. 6d. The Company was authorised to construct a standard gauge line passing along the Boulevard at Weston-super-Mare and continuing up Ashcombe Road. This street section of tramway was 37¼ chains in length. The Act only permitted passengers and their luggage on this section between 8 am and 8 pm unless the Company had the consent of the Weston-super-Mare Local Board. The 13 miles 64½ chains forming the remainder of the distance to Portishead was to follow an independent route through the open land and fields. The line along the Boulevard was to be double track, but the rest single.

It was intended that the River Yeo would be crossed by a combined rail and road bridge and it was hoped that this would prove to be a profitable sideline. Proposed tolls for the bridge were:

Horse drawn vehicle	6d.
Bicycle	3d.
Foot passenger	1d.

[53 & 54 Vict.] *Weston-super-Mare, Clevedon, and* **[Ch. cxxxii.]**
Portishead Tramways Act, 1890.

CHAPTER cxxxii.

An Act to extend the time limited for the completion of the A.D. 1890.
works authorised by the Weston-super-Mare Clevedon and
Portishead Tramways Act 1885 and for other purposes.
[25th July 1890.]

WHEREAS by the Weston-super-Mare Clevedon and Portishead
Tramways Act 1885 (in this Act called "the Act of 1885")
the Weston-super-Mare Clevedon and Portishead Tramways Company (in this Act called "the Company") were incorporated and
were authorised to construct the tramways with a new road and
bridge in connexion therewith in the county of Somerset in that
Act more particularly described :

And whereas by the Act of 1885 the time for the completion of
the works thereby authorised was limited to five years from the
passing of such Act which received the Royal Assent on the sixth
day of August one thousand eight hundred and eighty-five and it is
expedient that that time should be extended and that the Act of
1885 should be amended in manner herein-after provided :

And whereas the purposes of this Act cannot be effected without
the authority of Parliament :

May it therefore please Your Majesty that it may be enacted and
be it enacted by the Queen's most Excellent Majesty by and with
the advice and consent of the Lords Spiritual and Temporal and
Commons in this present Parliament assembled and by the authority
of the same as follows :—

1. This Act may be cited as the Weston-super-Mare Clevedon and   Short title.
Portishead Tramways Act 1890.

2. The provisions of Part II. (relating to extension of time) of   Incorpora-
the Railways Clauses Act 1863 are (except where expressly varied by   tion of Act.
this Act) incorporated with and form part of this Act and in con-
struing the provisions of that Act the expression "the railway"
[*Price* 6*d.*]

The first page of the Weston-super-Mare, Clevedon and Portishead Tramways Act of
1890.

In the event, the bridge was only open to railborne traffic.

The Act stipulated that persons and carriages on Her Majesty's service should be exempt from payment. This would have included members of the Royal Family, postmen, soldiers and sailors, customs officers and policemen, together with prisoners, if any! The Act warned the tramway company that no engine, carriage or wagon must obstruct traffic to the GWR station at Clevedon for longer than a reasonable time to allow passengers to get in or out of the carriages. In fact there was a penalty of 40 shillings for each offence and an additional sum of 40 shillings for every 15 minutes the offence continued.

The engines, trucks and carriages were not to extend more than 22 inches beyond the outer rail of the tramway on either side. The engines were required to have a suitable fender to push aside obstructions and a special bell or whistle. A seat had to be provided for the driver and the engine was to be 'free from noise produced by blast or clatter of machinery'. Moving parts had to be concealed from 4 inches above rail level and the fire hidden from view. In short, the usual type of tramway engine was required. The use of steam power was only sanctioned for seven years and for further periods of seven years if the Board of Trade agreed. Speed on the street tramway section was restricted to 8 mph, with a further restriction to 4 mph at facing points. To enable this to be observed, locomotives were required to be fitted with a speed indicator. It was stipulated that every engine 'shall have its number shown in some conspicuous part thereof', though early engines failed to comply with this ruling. Authorisation was also given to enter into agreements with the GWR for interchange traffic.

The capital of £60,000 was to be raised by shares of £10 each and borrowing powers of £15,000 were authorised. The six Directors were required to hold at least fifty shares. The Directors were: Sir Edmund Elton, Henry Daniel, Samuel Baker, Henry Wansbrough, John Griffin and one other to be nominated by them. Powers for compulsory purchase expired after three years and all works had to be completed within five years of the Act being passed. Although the Act stipulated that the first meeting of shareholders should have been within six months of incorporation, typical of the lax ways of the company it was not held until 12th July, 1886, at the company's offices at 70 Queen Square, Bristol. A. H. Wansbrough took the chair, with J. F. R. Daniel as Secretary; auditor was C. J. Ryland, holding the same position with the gas and water companies at Clevedon.

In May 1886 the Company issued a prospectus which pointed out that the transport of agricultural produce and stone from the quarries was to be as important as passenger carrying. It also stated that a provisional contract had been let to John Fell of Leamington, who was to build the line within six months of 'breaking ground'. The *Clevedon Mercury* amplified this statement adding that Fell's estimate was for £37,000, leaving £23,000 the balance of the authorised capital for purchase of land, locomotives and rolling stock. Arrangements had been made for the construction to proceed by sections, commencing with those in which agreements for possession of land on satisfactory terms could be 'most quickly' made. A dividend of as high as 7¼ per cent was expected, though this figure was gleaned from street

The Subscription List will be closed <u>on or before</u> Thursday, May 27th.

THE

WESTON-SUPER-MARE, CLEVEDON & PORTISHEAD (STEAM) TRAMWAYS COMPANY,

(With Junctions with the Great Western Railway.)

Incorporated by special Act of Parliament 48 and 49 Vict. Cap. 182, whereby the liability of each Shareholder is absolutely limited to the amount unpaid on his Subscription.

CAPITAL £60,000 IN 6,000 SHARES OF £10 EACH.

Payable £1 on application, £1 on allotment, and the balance in calls not exceeding £2, at intervals of not less than two months.

Directors :
Until the First Meeting of the Company.
SIR EDMUND HARRY ELTON, BART., *Chairman*, Clevedon Court, Somerset.
SAMUEL EDWARD BAKER, ESQ., Weston-super-Mare.
HENRY DANIEL, ESQ., Tyndall's Park, Clifton.
JOHN GRIFFIN, ESQ., Kenn, Somerset.
HENRY WANSBROUGH, ESQ., Weston-super-Mare.

Engineer :
F. C. STILEMAN, ESQ., C.E., Great George Street, Westminster.

Solicitors :
MESSRS. OSBORNE, WARD, VASSALL & Co., Bristol.

Bankers :
THE NATIONAL PROVINCIAL BANK OF ENGLAND, London, Bristol & Portishead.
STUCKEY'S BANKING COMPANY, Weston-super-Mare and Clevedon.

Brokers :
MESSRS. GODWIN & WALTER, 8, Finch Lane, London, E.C.

Secretary :
J. F. R. DANIEL, ESQ.
(Late Secretary and General Manager Bristol and Portishead Railway and Docks.)

Offices : (*Temporary*)
70, QUEEN'S SQUARE, BRISTOL, AND 21, THREADNEEDLE STREET, LONDON, E.C.

Agent :
MR. SAMUEL DAWES, Birklands, Clevedon, and High Street, Weston-super-Mare.

PROSTECTUS.

Title of the Company.
THE title of the Company, as incorporated by special Act of Parliament obtained in 1885, is "The Weston-super-Mare, Clevedon and Portishead Tramways Company."

Object of the Company.
The object of the Company is to construct and work, by locomotive power, a tramway 14 miles in length, for carriage of passengers and goods, on lands to be purchased by the Company, adjacent to and easily accessible from existing highways, between the important and increasing towns of Weston-super-Mare, Clevedon and Portishead, the intermediate villages and the large import docks and warehouses at Portishead; also to construct certain sections of Tramway upon public roads; and to build and maintain a bridge over the river Yeo, with road-approaches.

The advantages of the undertaking.
The advantages of this undertaking are very great, there being at present no direct railway or tramway communication between Portishead, Clevedon and Weston, the only route from Portishead to Weston being viâ Bristol, and though only 13 miles apart, a to and fro journey takes a longer time than between either place and London, more than ten times the distance.

The Weston-super-Mare, Clevedon & Portishead (Steam) Tramways Company Prospectus, dated 20th May, 1886.

Passenger Traffic.

With the facilities that *will* be given by this Tramway, it is estimated that the large population consisting of residents and visitors and inhabitants generally, of the rising watering-places of Weston, Clevedon, and Portishead, will give a constant passenger traffic, increasing with the development at various points of the route of the numerous beautiful building sites now unavailable for want of access, while the picturesque nature of the country through which the line passes will insure a large tourist traffic.

Portishead as a Port, and Goods Traffic to and from it.

Portishead, with its fine docks and warehouses, is so naturally the port of this part of the West of England, that cheap and easy transit of goods by this Tramway, together with the collection of agricultural produce for the Town markets, the carriage of building materials, and the development of the valuable mines and quarries of the district will provide a steady paying and increasing goods traffic.

Suitableness of a Steam Tramway.

For these kinds of traffic a Steam Tramway near, but not running on the roads is the best that can be provided having regard to cheapness of construction, working, time, and convenience.

Cost of Construction and probable Profits.

The cost of construction, £3,000 per mile, exclusive of land, is less than one-tenth of the average cost of English railways, and less than one-third that of street tramways, while even upon that cost most of the latter are yielding good dividends. The average receipts per mile are very nearly as much for tramways as for railways.

Taking the capital expenditure of this undertaking at £60,000, and the gross receipts at one-third only of those averaged by the tramways of the United Kingdom, and making a liberal reduction for working expenses, it is calculated that the dividend earned should be at the rate of at least $7\frac{1}{2}$ per cent., which it is fair to presume will be increased upon the natural development of the traffic.

Estimate of traffic by comparison with that of the Bristol and Portishead Railway.

The Bristol and Portishead Railway (now taken over by the Great Western Railway Company), 10 miles in length, and having cost about £30,000 per mile, earned over £550 per month, from the time the first train was run; similar receipts per mile on this Tramway line, with its small cost of construction and working, would give enough to pay 10 per cent. dividends. Previous to the construction of the Bristol and Portishead Railway, the only public conveyance to Bristol was an Omnibus, which at present is the means of transit between Portishead and Clevedon.

Special reasons for the exceptional cheapness of construction and working.

There are no cuttings or embankments, and the gradients are practically level throughout, the line running through most picturesque valleys. There are also no Stations, and only one Bridge (this being over the River Yeo), which, in itself, will be a great boon to the district, providing much required means of transit over that portion of the river, and it is estimated that the tolls (as allowed by Act of Parliament) will of themselves produce a revenue sufficient to pay interest on the capital expended on the Bridge, which will be approached by a new Road to be constructed by the Company. The cost of traction is very small, as compared either with Railway, Road Omnibus, or Horse Tramways, and the terminal and staff expenses will be trifling. In practice the Tramcar stops whenever and only when passengers have to be taken up or set down.

Special arrangement with Great Western Railway.

Junctions with the Great Western Railway have been agreed upon, and the Tramway line is in other respects constructed to take ordinary Railway Rolling Stock, so that the traffic between Railway and Tramway will be easily interchanged.

Special feature of the Company.

This economical class of Steam Tramway running on its own land, and combining, at the low cost above mentioned, the most valuable advantages of a Railway and Tramway, is a new departure in locomotion, and certain to have a great future.

Contractor's agreement to complete, and prospect of early dividends.

A Contract has been entered into with Mr. JOHN FELL, of Leamington, the well known Tramway Contractor, who agrees to complete the line for the cost above stated, within six months from the date of commencement, when the Company will be in a position to begin earning dividends.

Preliminary expenses.

The preliminary expenses of the Company are limited to the actual outlay incurred in obtaining the Act of Parliament, &c.

Act of Parliament.

The Special Act of Parliament, &c., can be inspected at the Offices of the Company's Solicitors and Brokers.

Stock Exchange Quotation and Settlement, &c. &c.

A settlement and quotation on the Stock Exchange will be applied for in due course.

If no allotment is made the deposit will be returned in full.

Prospectus and forms of application may be had at the Bankers and Brokers.

Dated *May 20th*, 1886.

tramway returns, very different from the rural WCPT. The Company met with difficulties over acquisition of land, many owners being dissatisfied with the terms offered, thus forcing a series of arbitrations adding to both delay and cost. On 3rd July, 1886 the *Clevedon Mercury* reported: 'The Engineer and contractor of this line (WCPT) will walk the route on Monday week (12th July) for the purpose of making arrangements for the commencement of works'.

It is not known why Fell dropped out, but Messrs W. Gradwell of Barrow-in-Furness took over the contract by 20th September, 1887 when £11,681 had been subscribed. Work started at the Clevedon end of the line, rails and fastenings having been delivered and the line pegged out. The firm of McLean & Stileman, the WCPT's Engineers, were represented on the spot by Edward Thompson, Resident Engineer. The 27th of February, 1888 saw the SS *Dalriada* unloading at Clevedon Pill the first batch of 25,000 sleepers required, then the death of Gradwell caused work to come to a halt for over a year. By 1889 the WCPT Secretary was Edgar Bruce Ranald Daniel, J. F. R.'s second son. In 1885 J. F. R. had become general manager of the Midland & South Western Junction Railway and his eldest son, Arthur Francis Ranald Daniel, Secretary of the MSWJR. It is quite possible that J. F. R., the WCPT's general manager gave less attention to that line than he should have done, due to his many other interests elsewhere.

In March 1889 it was announced that Messrs Wilkinson & Co. of London were to start work immediately, the terms of their contract requiring the entire line from the Boulevard in Weston-super-Mare to the junction with the GWR at Portishead to be complete and ready for opening by October that year, subject to any short postponement due to delay in the WCPT gaining possession of land; while the section between Weston and Clevedon was to be opened if possible on 1st July. This was wishful thinking indeed and work had not started when Francis Stileman, Engineer, died on 18th May.

1889 saw the appointment of a new Chairman, Lt Col Sir Nicholas W. Elphinstone, Bt, *Times* correspondent during the 1870 Franco–Prussian War. Although by September 1889 20 navvies were at work and a section of line laid, only £15,696 had been subscribed. In November a new prospectus was published which sought to raise a further £42,500 and led to a sarcastic critique in the *Financial News* of 22nd November.

THE LITTLE WESTERN

We present the above title free, *gratis*, and for nothing to the Weston-super-Mare, Clevedon, and Portishead Tramways Company. We have already a North Western, and in the earlier ages of railway history we had a Little North Western. We have a Great Western; why not, then, also a Little Western? Our only hesitation is whether it should not more accurately be called 'The Least Western'; for, indeed, it is a most modest and retiring little line. The mortals, therefore, who are so fortunate as to be shareholders in both Great and Little Western simultaneously will be able, unlike the rest of mankind, to eat their cake and have it too. As Great Western shareholders, they will gain by the abstraction of their present traffic; in their Little Western capacity they will reap the full benefit, not only of the haulage of the present traffic, but of all the vast increase that the future has in store. For the line is being 'constructed on the same gauge as the Great Western' that is, apparently, though the prospectus does not specify, on the mixed gauge of both 7 ft and 4 ft 8½ in. [the paper erred here] — 'and in such a substantial manner, that the Great Western rolling stock can, without any transhipment, be hauled by ordinary locomotives'. Every railway man will at once perceive what a profitable undertaking it must be to haul Great Western rolling-stock without transhipment. Nay, more, 'there will be sidings to quarries of pennant and other stone used for building, paving, etc., and quarries of limestone used for refining, etc., which, up to now, the want of railway facilities has prevented from being brought into the market'. Conceive the future that lies open before a line which can bring sidings and quarries in wholesale quantities into the market, and all for a capital cost, 'exclusive of land', of £4000 per mile.

Still, investors, and especially old ladies and the country parsons to whom the present golden opportunity is afforded, are proverbially shy, and it is, perhaps, conceivable that the whole of the £42,500 may not be subscribed by the Great Western shareholders, or, at least that 'the premium offered for the same' may not be sufficient in the opinion of the directors. Some portion of the amount may accordingly find its way next week into the open market. We think, therefore, that, before recommending the investment to our readers, we ought to clear up one or two points which are not as distinct as we would wish them to be. The Weston-super-Mare is, we are told, 'being constructed as an ordinary railway' and yet we also learn that among the items of capital expenditure saved are 'cost of stations, platforms, signals, telegraphs, and road-bridges', and that on revenue account there will be nothing to pay for 'wages of station-masters, clerks, porters, signalmen and gatekeepers', or for the 'maintenance of stations, signals, bridges, etc.' Surely this is not an ordinary, but a most extraordinary railway. What railway contemplates earning £67 per mile per week — 'the average amount earned on railways', without stations and without signals; possibly, on the other hand, the directors have bought up a job lot second-hand, and propose to present them to their company *gratis*. Then we are not quite clear as to the important matter of land. We are told in one place that 'the line will be on the company's own freehold land', in another, that there will be an 'annual rent-charge of £200, granted in payment for land, ranking for dividend before the ordinary shares'. Really, the freehold of the company seems to be of a kind so limited and qualified as to satisfy the most radical land-law reformer.

. . . we know nothing whatever of the undertaking beyond what appears on the prospectus. It is possible that it is both an honest and a promising one. If so, its directors have only themselves to thank if they find it looked upon as a dishonest and bogus one.

. . . when the public are invited to subscribe on the face of a prospectus which pretends that an ordinary railway can be built at £4000 a mile, which compares the earnings of an agricultural tram line with those of a trunk railroad plus those of a metropolitan tramway, it is only possible to acquit the directors of deliberate imposition by supposing them lacking in ordinary intelligence. And be the explanation of their action the one or the other, they are not persons to whom any sane human being would entrust his money for investment.

Some unrevealed difficulties were experienced with the contractors and this delayed works, but differences were settled in the spring of 1890 and it was anticipated the line would be ready within a year. Cash trickled in and May saw fencing completed between Clevedon and Wick St Lawrence, while the same month a contractor's locomotive worked seven or eight times daily between Clevedon and Kingston Seymour. June saw timber scaffolding for the Yeo Bridge arrive from Newport and 10,000 sleepers being landed at

Clevedon Pill at the far end of Old Church Road, while the stone bridge across the Land Yeo near Clevedon station was 'being rapidly pushed on'. Conservation was not overlooked, the *Clevedon Mercury* of 7th June, 1890 reporting that the beautiful chestnut tree on land between Queen's Road and Kenn Road was not to be felled. It also reported the probability of a large brick yard being opened by a Welsh firm near the Yeo Bridge, though in the event this was not to be. The paper rather ambitiously announced that the opening to Weston-super-Mare was contemplated in September. It also published a statement later to be disproved, 'The line itself gives evidence of substantial workmanship'.

The five years allowed by the Act for completing the line had expired and another Act, 53 & 54 Vic. cap. 132 of 25th July, 1890 was passed for the extension of time and other purposes. The period allowed for completion was extended by one year from 6th August, 1890. Furthermore, this new Act allowed trains to be driven by electric power and in this event, provision was made to protect the lines of the Western Counties and South Wales Telephone Company and the telegraph lines of the Postmaster General should this form of traction have been adopted.

By now Henry Jackson of London had the contract and in May 1891 metalwork for the Yeo Bridge was ready for delivery. The time allowed by the second Act for completion was expiring and a Bill for further extension was deposited on 21st December, 1891. The company said it was unable to complete the line, or purchase the remainder of the land, 'in consequence of financial difficulties, and especially of the failure of parties and firms with whom the company had made contracts'; so stated the preamble to the Act of 27th July, 1892, 55 & 56 Vic. cap. 158. It was thought that a connection with the GWR would be to the public's advantage. Powers granted in the 1885 Act were revived, and also the construction of junctions with the GWR at both Weston-super-Mare and Portishead was authorised. At Weston there was to be a line 2 furlongs 9.55 chains in length from Worle to the GWR's Weston-super-Mare loop line and at Portishead a branch of 7.65 chains to the GWR branch. Although this Act made it rather more a railway than tramway, level crossings being gated and track reserved and fenced, the title remained unaltered.

One section stated that 'whereas the tramroads will not be laid along public roads' the rules in the schedule of the 1885 Act would not apply and that the level crossings over public roads must have gates, but the 10 mph limit would still be in force. The company was not allowed to use 'any trucks or carriages other than tramroad passenger cars' on the street tramway section in Weston and carry no goods traffic except passengers' baggage and Royal Mail in this street section. If the local highway board required, in the parishes of Kingston Seymour, Walton-in-Gordano and Portishead, screens were to be erected on both sides of the highway to prevent engines and trains from scaring horses. The Act allowed two years for the tramway to be completed between Weston and Clevedon and a junction made at Worle with the GWR; and four years for the section from Clevedon to Portishead to be built and the junction with the GWR installed at the latter town. In order that the company could complete the line and raise money for extra works, powers were given for an additional capital of £20,000, together with borrowing powers of £5000, though none of this extra capital could be raised until the line was opened between Clevedon and Weston. The Act also provided for the WCPT to be taken over by the GWR and authorised the latter company to raise additional capital for this purpose.

21st June, 1894 saw the contractors laying the street section in Milton Road, omitting to give the local authority the necessary plans and seven days notice as required by the 1870 Street Tramways Act, but their apology and explanation was accepted. That summer a vessel from South Wales arrived at the New Year Slip, Wick St Lawrence, loaded with rails and sleepers, while Messrs Lysaght of Bristol were assembling the Yeo Bridge. The half-yearly report for February 1896 recorded that the contractor, Messrs Jackson, had run a locomotive and seven ballast wagons over the bridge.

In July 1896 the WCPT approached British Electric Traction with a view to selling, but the price of £45,000 for the almost-completed line was too high for the latter to be interested. In 1898 overhead electric wires were not allowed on the WCPT, but the BET planned to begin with steam if it took the line over, and obtain an Order for wires later. On the WCPT becoming a light railway, the BET still considered taking over the concern since it already held some financial interest. The railway was thoroughly investigated, but an agreeable price could not be struck and a complete purchase was never made.[1]

Notes:

1. BET File WCM 81T 1898–1912

A static view of *Clevedon* at Portishead in 1907 with its new more enclosed cab. The passenger stock consists of the 3-coach 'Metropolitan' set – later these vehicles were used in sets of two.   *Author's Collection*

Locomotive *Weston* seen here at Clevedon, with train for Weston-super-Mare, c.1900. Notice the very low timber platform seen in this view towards the buffers. The GWR goods shed is to the right of the smokebox door. *Courtesy Railway Magazine*

A typical cattle grid on the WC&PT c.1899. The notice reads 'WC&PT Trespassers will be Prosecuted'. *Author's Collection*

Chapter Three
Construction Continues

Shareholders were told at their meeting in December 1896[1] that the contractor had signed an agreement to complete his work in order to obtain the Board of Trade Certificate within six weeks. Extra navvies were taken on and in one day 100 tons of material was drawn over the line to Weston-super-Mare. The Urban District Council at Weston instructed the clerk to give the company notice 'to remove so much of their rails as have been laid or buried in the streets within the council's district', suggesting the railway type rail with clamped on check rail be replaced by that of the tramway pattern which had a smaller gap and was therefore better for road users, but the company found this suggestion unacceptable.

In May 1897 Jackson stopped work, probably through lack of payment as the company still owed him money in 1905. Completion of the line was carried out by the company's own staff under the supervision of William Cox of Clevedon and Edward Wintour, traffic manager and locomotive superintendent. The first recorded run from Clevedon to Weston-super-Mare was on 18th August, 1897. It consisted of a single car drawn by the contractor's 0–4–0ST nicknamed 'Coffee Pot'. This having proved a success another trip was made the following day, the *Weston Gazette*[2] recording:

> On Thursday (19th August) Mr Daniels of Portishead (managing director of the company), Mr Loxton, Mr Wintour, (traffic manager), and several other gentlemen and ladies, made a trial trip over the route to Weston, a carriage having already also run through the day before. The train consisted of three cars and an engine, being of first and second class and well finished. They are 50 feet long and have seating accommodation for 60 people each. The seats are of American bent wood, and run lengthwise, with communication from end to end, while the first class of blue velvet upholstery, have seats facing the engine. The journey is divided into eight penny per mile stages — one shilling return — with stoppages where necessary, and the run from Clevedon averages about 20 minutes each way. The carriages ran very smoothly, the only incident worth noting being the alarm of the cattle *en route* at the puffing of the engine. When in full working order, the line should have an important bearing upon the busy agricultural district through which it runs, besides doing much to facilitate intercourse and business transactions between the two towns. The inspection by the Board of Trade will take place next week, after which it is expected that this portion of line will be opened for use of the travelling public. The line to Portishead is not likely to be taken in hand for some little time. A great convenience, when the completed portion is in working order, should be the workmen's train each way at the rate of a halfpenny per mile.

Sir Francis Marindin, RE, KCMG, visited the line on behalf of the Board of Trade on 28th August and made his report[3] and it is interesting to note that he used the old form of the letter 's'.

> 28 August 1897
> SIR, I have the honour to report for the information of the Board of Trade, that in compliance with the instructions contained in your Minute of the 6 Inst. I have inspected the completed portion of the Weston-super-Mare, Clevedon and Portishead Tramways, for which an Act was obtained in 1885, but which are being constructed under the powers of an Act of 1892.
>   The line now submitted for inspection is that portion of Tramway No. 2 which lies between Weston-super-Mare and Clevedon and it has a length of 8m 6ch.

The line is single throughout, but there are loops at each end, and at two intermediate places, and a siding connection at another intermediate point. It runs entirely thro' fields, but crosses 13 public roads on the level. It is with very little exception a surface line thro' a flat country, with no steep gradients and it is, generally speaking, straight or nearly so.

The permanent way consists of Vignolles Rails (sic), weighing 60 lbs per yard, fished at the joints and secured to transom half round sleepers of Baltic timber by Dog spikes and 3 fang bolts for each rail.

The ballast is broken stone and the line is fenced in accordance with the Act. Part of the fencing is of old quick hedges with ditches, but the new fencing is wire fencing. There is one bridge over the River Yeo with seven spans of 30 feet, 10 other bridges over streams and drains, and 1 cattle creep, but there are no other bridges. The River Yeo Bridge has spans of cast iron screw piles and longitudinal girders of wrt. iron. The other bridges have each only one span varying from 12 ft to 30 ft in width. Five have steel girders and five have cast iron girders and in all cases the abutments are of masonry.

These bridges, or most of them, have been built for a number of years, and under these circumstances and considering the nature of the line, I do not think that the use of the cast iron girders need be objected, provided they are of sufficiently strong section. They are to all appearances, but as no particulars of the Engines which are to be used to work the line were forthcoming I am unable to state so positively. All the girders gave satisfactory results when tested with a small contractor's Engine and some Railway trucks loaded with stone.

The permanent way has been in places laid for many years and a great number of bad sleepers have been taken out, some sections having been entirely re-sleepered.

There are, however, a number still remaining on the road which are not fit to be run over, and which must be replaced by new sleepers before the line can be certified as fit for traffic.

There is on the line at most places a sufficiency of ballast, but it is in many places not properly distributed, and a great deal of packing up, and straightening is required.

The fencing also requires attention in many places, especially some of the old quick fencing where gaps must be made good.

According to the Act — Section 10 — there are to be gates across the Tramway, or Tramroad, at all the public road level crossings, but none of these have yet been fixed.

There are no signals on the line, and no buildings of any description.

There are 6 specially constructed long bogie cars, with platforms at each end, so that no station platforms are necessary, but the Act allows ordinary Railway Carriages on the Tramway and if this be done, some platforms will be required at the stopping places.

There is no limit of speed under the Act except at the crossing of public roads, where the speed is not to exceed 10 miles an hour.

It is proposed to work the line at first with one Engine in steam, but the Engines, apart from the contractor's, have not yet been delivered.

All the passenger stock is fitted with the automatic vacuum brake.

The following are the requirements which I noted —

1. The fixing of the gates at the Level Crossings.
2. The removal of all rotten sleepers and the improvement of the condition of the permanent way where pointed out.
3. The making good of all gaps in the fencing.
4. The provision of a buffer stop at the commencement of the line at Weston-super-Mare, and the removal of a length of rails which are left on the public footpath.

5. Brick parts at the fences at some of Rhine (a drain) bridges are necessary.
6. The possession of proper Engines to work the line. According to the Act these Engines should consume their own smoke, but so long as the line is not along public roads, this is not of much importance. As, however, the Engines are second hand, some particulars as to their history should be given and a certificate from some competent person that they are in good working order, especially in regard to their boilers and fireboxes, should be forthcoming.
7. A shelter shed of a simple character at each end of the line is necessary.

Until the first six of these requirements are satisfied I am unable to recommend the Board of Trade to grant a certificate that the line is fit for traffic, but if a good gang of experienced platelayers is set to work at once it ought not to take long to get the line into proper running order when a re-inspection should be made. It will, however, be necessary, either to limit the speed to 15 miles an hour, or to require some simple safety appliances at the facing points of the loops, and if at some future time more than one engine is brought into use and trains are passed at these loops and the speed is increased, a certain amount of signalling will be necessary.

In the meantime giving an undertaking to work with one engine only in steam and to limit the speed to 15 miles an hour might be accepted as sufficient.

I have the honour to be Sir
Your servant
F. A. Marindin
Maj. RE

J. F. R. Daniel, Managing Director of the WCPT replied to Marindin's report by saying that about two dozen level crossing gates were found at Clevedon. No one knew what they were for, or to whom they belonged. They now knew that they belonged to the tramway and were being erected.

Marindin also received a letter from a solicitor saying that fences were only 2½ ft high in places and a client of his was worried because should a beast be knocked down, the impecunious state of the company would prevent damages being paid.

Weston-super-Mare Urban District Council sent Marindin a letter observing that the rails of the street tramway section protruded above the road surface and were dangerous. They pointed out that the WCPT had also omitted to repair the roadway between the rails and for 18 inches on either side as required by the Act. The council itself had carried out repairs, but so far had not been reimbursed by the company. At a council meeting on 8th September, 1897 it was reported that Daniel, as Secretary to the WCPT, had written informing the council that rails laid in Ashcombe Road, Milton Road, Gerard Road and the Boulevard would be removed at once and the roadways made good. He added that the company was not prepared to propose any other form of new rail than that already submitted and rejected by the council, but suggested that the Bristol pattern of street rail should be put down. The council declined to discuss the question of arrangement with the company until the existing rails were lifted and the outstanding debt paid.

In view of the impending opening of the tramway in September (as they hoped) the company purchased the end houses Nos. 18 and 20 in Lower Queen's Road, Clevedon. The former was used for staff and office accommodation, the latter transferred from Bristol, the booking office being in the ground floor front room. No. 20 eventually had to be demolished to allow the line to be extended to Portishead.

About eighty prominent Westonians including members of the Urban District Council received an invitation for a free trip to Clevedon on 7th October. On this day the run from Weston to Clevedon took 35 minutes. The train was again pulled by the contractor's engine and was driven by no less a personage than the manager of the line Edward Wintour, dressed in a knickerbocker suit. A contemporary account of the excursion read:

> The trip was uneventful though highly enjoyable and within 25 minutes of the start, the passengers alighted at Clevedon, loud in their expression of approval as to the manner in which the run had been taken.

A later writer revealed that this description belied the truth. The engine was brought to a stand on the Yeo bridge so that passengers could admire the view and after a suitable pause, failed to start. She was put into reverse and then started easily. Apparently the more ribald passengers remarked afterwards that there was a falling off in speed every time the whistle blew.

The WCPT was very keen on the merits of advance publicity and invited the residents along the line to join an afternoon excursion on 23rd October. The party from Weston numbered more than a hundred and all were invited to tea at the Bristol Hotel, Clevedon, by Mr James Cook of Weston-super-Mare. Three cars were used on this occasion and the journey took 27 minutes each way.

Col Addison carried out the Board of Trade re-inspection on 9th November, making the following report:[4]

Nov 17th 1897

SIR, I have the honour to report for the information of the Board of Trade, that in compliance with the instructions contained in your Minute of the 23rd Octr. I have re-inspected the Weston-S-Mare and Clevedon tramroad (for Sir F. Marindin) with refce. to the requirements contained in the report of Aug. 28 '97 R10528.

The road is now in fair order for a line of this description, but there are still places, here and there, where, as I pointed out, it will still be necessary to pack up the ballast under the sleepers — to prevent movement which would soon loosen the fastenings of the rails. A large amount of extra ballast has been put on the line, and a considerable number of new sleepers (of rectangular section) have been laid.

The fencing has been made good where necessary, except at Clevedon station where further repairs are needed. The fencing is of a very light type, but I am not prepared to say it is unsuitable for the purpose for which it is intended.

Level crossing gates. Gates have now been erected. They only fence the tramroad, and not the public road (when open) as usual in the case of railways, it would however appear that this is all the company are called upon to do under clause 10 of their Act (1892). The gate posts have only a clearance varying from 2 ft 5 in. to 2 ft 2 in. from the rails, which would be quite insufficient to provide proper safety if ordinary, passenger, railway carriages be at any time used on the line. So long as the tramway type of vehicle is used no objection need, I think, be raised to the present arrangts.

N.B. It has already been pointed out by Sir F. Marindin that if ordinary railway carriages are used the question of platforms will have to be dealt with also.

Buffer stops. These have been provided at both ends of the line, and the old rails laid in the street, and across the footpath, at Weston have been taken up.

Shelter Sheds. These are not yet erected, but I was informed that they have been ordered.

Owing to the girders of the bridge over the river Yeo being somewhat weak, (theoretically) and to the existence (as pointed out by Sir F. Marindin) of a number of old cast iron bridges on the line I can only recommend the Board of Trade to issue a certificate that the tramroad is fit for traffic if *the weight to be carried on any axle be limited to 10 tons.* The following conditions are also necessary to ensure safety:

1. The maximum speed should not exceed 15 miles an hour until such time as:
   (a) continuous brakes are in use on all passenger vehicles, capable of being applied by the engine driver and guard.
   (b) all facing points are fitted with safety appliances.

   Further, until the above be complied with not more than one vehicle should be run on a train, with a man to attend to the hand brake, and the facing points should be secured and left out of use.
2. The Company shd. undertake to work the line with one Engine in steam (or two coupled together).
3. Tramway type of carriage to be used.

It would probably be advisable for the Company's Engineer to arrange a meeting with the Inspecting Officers, to discuss the details of the arrangements to be made in refce. to the facing connections of loops or sidings — which need only be of a simple description. It would, also I think, tend to simplify matters very much if the passenger road at Clevedon were made to the left, instead of the right, hand line of rails (approaching Clevedon from Weston).

Details of the Engines to be used on the line have yet to be furnished.

I have etc.,
G. W. Addison
Lt Col RE

P.S. Since the above report was written I have recd. the enclosed particulars of the engine which the Company wish to commence running, pending the completion of an engine for permanent use on the line. Cl. 27(b) of the 1892 Act does not appear to me to require the Board of Trade to inspect the locomotives, and the only question at present involved is that of the weight on the wheels. The engine referred to in the attached correspondence complies with the requirement I have made that the weight on any axle is not to exceed 10 tons. The engine would also appear to be in a fit state for use. (I have dealt in the report with the question of brakes.)

P.P.S. It might be well to point out to the Company that should they, at any future time, run through the streets of Weston or Clevedon etc. it wd. be necessary for them to use the ordinary and usual type of tramway engines.

G.W.A.

Harold, a Kitson 0−6−0 saddle tank locomotive hired from Mackay & Davies, was the engine to work the line for the first month or six weeks, the company's engine *Clevedon* built by Walker Brothers being under repair. A report on its condition was given by the GWR locomotive superintendent at Newport. On 29th November the WCPT made a written undertaking to carry out within three months the Board of Trade inspecting officer's requirements mentioned above.

The *Bristol Mercury* displayed little enthusiasm over the public opening on 1st December, its section on Clevedon news giving only 'The tramway connecting this town with Weston-super-Mare was opened to the public on Wednesday. Several persons availed themselves of the opportunity of travelling over the new line'.

The *Clevedon Mercury*[5] showed much more enthusiasm.

THE LIGHT RAILWAY TO WESTON-SUPER-MARE
FIRST IMPRESSIONS

Punctuality, civility, at the start; moderate speed, with steadiness on the road, and on this occasion, at all events, plenty of room to promenade from end to end, as on an American railway.

To find oneself drifting through a new district, though it be but meadow land, some of it dotted with elm timber and orchards, enlivened by the scampering of young cattle or colts, is of itself a new pleasure.

The pretty part is after passing the Yeo Bridge, Wick St Lawrence, with its square tower on the right. You skirt under the south side of Worle Hill, and arrive at a part of Weston which leads down the Boulevard straight into the town.

No doubt in time the officials will provide their passengers with guide books of this little line; which will give hints of many possibilities for the pedestrian or pleasure seeker.

For instance: With my small knowledge of the locality I lay out for myself or my friends to 'descend' as the French say, at Worle, walk over and along the top of the hill by the old windmill (now a residence), breathe the invigorating air of the Channel, and walk as far as Weston.

Or round the near end of the hill, and take the road under its north side to Kewstoke, inspect the church, and proceed through the wood to the pier end of Weston.

From Worle also it is no very long walk to Woodspring Priory — a spot full of interest, though not often visited. When there let your thoughts go back to the days when the monks and recluses luxuriated amongst its pastures and stately elms.

With a cup of mine host's tea, bread and butter and cream, you will be refreshed, so as to turn your steps back through Wick St Lawrence, and meet the tram a little beyond.

On a summer's afternoon, a walk from near the Priory along the sea wall of something over a mile, catch the tram on the bridge over the Yeo, and home.

Many other 'lifts' for the walker may be found — such as to Kingston Seymour, or to the lane which leads to the skating ponds. But these are enough to wet [sic] the appetite for a cheap and easy trip.

In writing this, understand I have no interest whatever in this tramway company. But it certainly will be one of the additional pleasures of Clevedon in the summer and at this time of the year may be a means of relieving the monotony incident to winter wherever you may be.

Fred F. Cottrell

Clevedon 3rd December 1897.

The first public trip of the new steam tramway between Clevedon and Weston-super-Mare was run on Wednesday December 1st at two o'clock. There are eight penny stages, the return fare being 1s. Mr J. F. R. Daniel of Portishead, managing director, accompanied the party. The return journey occupied little over an hour and it is anticipated that the average time taken when everything is got into thorough working order will be about half an hour each way. A good number of Portishead enthusiasts arrived at Clevedon by special buses to take part in the public trip. It is hoped that the extension of the tram line to Portishead will soon be commenced.[6]

The tramway quickly got into its stride and special late trains were run between Clevedon and Weston on 21st December in connection with a meat and poultry show at the latter town. On Boxing Day the line carried 1254 passengers, while 500 availed themselves of its services the following day.

Except on Sundays an omnibus owned by the WCPT met all trains at Weston running to Birnbeck Pier thus facilitating traffic to and from the sea front and also round trip excursions from South Wales to Weston Pier, over the tramway between Weston and Clevedon, and from Clevedon Pier back by sea to South Wales. The pleasure steamers belonged to Messrs P. & A. Campbell's White Funnel Fleet and from 1908 until 1910 also those of the Red Funnel Line, owned by the Barry Railway.

Portishead was connected with the tramway at Clevedon by Brown's horse omnibus and through tickets were issued from Portishead to Weston at the return fare of two shillings. Brown's had operated the service for many years and was simply modified to connect with trains. Richard Stephens built several cars at Clevedon, one being the first 'Motor omnibus' which carried nine passengers and ran between Clevedon and Portishead for two shillings return. This service ceased in 1906.

On 11th December, 1897 J. F. R. Daniel wrote[7] to the Board of Trade asking for a relaxation of the ruling that trains should consist of only one vehicle quoting the following figures to show overcrowding occurred on some occasions:

	Time of Train	No. of passengers
Saturday 4th December, 1897	2.00 pm	128
	2.45	37
	4.00	51
	6.50	61
	8.45	73
Sunday 5th December, 1897	2.00	47
	4.00	40
	4.45	49
	6.00	38

In support of his claim Daniel said that the car brakes had been improved so that they worked on all eight wheels. The Board of Trade agreed to a maximum of two coaches being used as long as the company agreed to fit continuous brakes within three months and on condition that a brakesman whose sole duty was to attend to the brakes, was on each car. On 22nd December, 1897 the agreement for fitting continuous brakes was signed and sealed.

It is interesting that for the first six months of 1899 locomotive power cost £516 and horses for the bus £298, that is more than half the locomotive costs.

By 6th May, 1898, it was reported that one newly-ordered engine was on the line (this would have been either the Walker Brothers *Clevedon* or the Robert Stephenson *Portishead* both of which were 0-6-0 tank engines) and the other expected within a week. A loop had been built midway between the terminii in order that trains could pass each other. On 12th May, 1898 Colonel Addison made his report[8] on this loop at Wick St Lawrence which had an available length of nearly 100 yds and short overshoot roads at either end. The points were worked from ground levers controlled by Annett's locks. The turnout was locked open to the left hand road and could only be opened by Annett's key on the staff belonging to the section ahead. Col Addison thought it advisable that the key be made an integral part of the train staff instead of being separate.

Small automatic semaphore signals showed when the line had been set for trains to run out of the loop. They were at danger when the points were replaced and until this was done, the key could not be removed. There were no signal lamps, but the powerful acetylene headlights on the engine brightly illuminated the track ahead for 150 yards and enabled drivers to see the signals. Addison thought it a novel arrangement and said it might be given a trial on the distinct understanding that the usual lamps would be fixed if the Board of Trade required. He passed the loop so long as only one engine in steam (or two coupled together), were allowed in each section carrying the staff of the section in which the train was travelling. He did not consider the speed limit should be increased until sidings at each end of the line, like the intermediates, had facing point locks controlled by Annett's key, adding 'it will also be necessary for the company to undertake to have continuous brakes in actual operation on all vehicles carrying passengers'.

Towards the end of 1898 the employees of the WCPT celebrated the success of the line by a dinner given by mine host, Thomas Ascott of the Bristol Hotel, Clevedon.

Notes:

1. *Clevedon Mercury*, 12th December, 1896
2. *Weston Gazette*, 21st August, 1897
3. Public Record Office: MT6/2484/5
4. PRO: MT6/2484/5
5. *Clevedon Mercury*, 4th December, 1897
6. *Ibid*
7. PRO: MT6/2484/5
8. *Ibid*

A broadside view of *Weston* and its train, again posed for an official photograph on the Wick St Lawrence bridge, *c.*1899.   *Author's Collection*

Chapter Four
Extension to Portishead

When in 1889 the plans for the tramway were being prepared, many protests were received from residents in the beautiful East Clevedon valley, against the tramway passing near All Saints' Church and schools. The Clevedon Urban District Council strongly opposed level crossings on the extension foreseeing inconvenience and danger if the tramway crossed the road in front of the GWR's Clevedon station. Even before the Weston to Clevedon section was open, the CUDC opposed the extension and it was quite in order for them to do so as the tramway company's powers had lapsed. The CUDC held a long debate in February 1899 and decided to oppose the extension bill, the cost of opposition being charged to the general district rates.

Primary objections were that the extra level crossings would be detrimental to building developments and the frequent whistling of engines would detract from the local amenities. The level crossings were thought dangerous and certainly around that period level crossing accidents were common all over the country.

A census was taken to prove how busy the proposed crossing of Kenn Road–Station Road was. In inclement weather on 4th February, 4442 pedestrians and 828 vehicles passed over between 8 am and 8 pm. On 7th February, 4696 pedestrians and 848 vehicles were counted. Chairman of the council, Sir Edmund Elton, said the council had to foresee the time when the GWR would take over the tramway and run heavy goods and passenger services on it. The Commissioner of Sewers from the Wrington Division of Somerset was afraid that bridges would diminish the capacity of the waterways in flood time.

The WCPT Engineer undaunted, went ahead and estimated the cost of the line, including the GWR junction at Portishead, to be £20,258. In May 1899 the Bill came before the Select Committee of the House of Lords presided over by Lord Brougham. On 9th June, 1899 at the shareholders' meeting it was announced that in the second half year's working, receipts were £2682 and expenses £1601. A dividend of 4 per cent on preference shares was adopted.

An Act of 9th August, 1899, 62 & 63 Vic. cap. 221, authorised the conversion of the existing tramway to a light railway and a change of name to the Weston, Clevedon & Portishead Light Railway Company, the concern becoming one of the very few working under its own Act instead of a Light Railway Order. Despite the change of name, people at West Huish still referred to the line as the 'tramway' and said that they went into Weston 'by tram'.

The junction with the GWR at Weston was abandoned, together with the street tramway, and under this new Act, a light railway from Clevedon to Portishead, a distance of 5 miles 67 chains, was authorised, together with an end-on junction with a GWR siding at Portishead which was about 8 chains distant from the WCPT terminus. Five years were allowed for the work, together with the task of making the existing tramway into a light railway. Gates under the 1892 Act could be removed, except at three crossings near

Locomotive *Portishead* with a train from Portishead approaching Clevedon Triangle on the 10th August, 1935. The crossing gate behind the lady cyclist's head only covers about half the road. The hinged section to cover the remainder has not been unfolded. *R.W. Kidner*

Locomotive No. 3 *Weston* crossing the road at Clevedon outside the W.H. Smith Circulating Library with train to Portishead on the 13th July, 1935. *S.W. Baker*

Worle, and gates on the extension would be required only at Clevedon and
Portishead. At each ungated crossing there was to be a white post 300 yds
either side along the railway bearing a 5 ft high board carrying a figure, being
the restriction in miles per hour. Fifty yards along the road on either side, a
'Beware of the Trains' sign had to be erected. Running rails at the crossing
were required to be guarded by a cattle grid.

An interesting new restriction appeared in the Act.

> It shall not be lawful for any engine, carriage, wagon or other vehicle using the
> railway to pass over the level crossing in Clevedon in front of the GWR passenger
> station within 10 minutes after arrival or before the departure of any GWR pas-
> senger train to ensure safe working of road traffic to and from the station.

Furthermore a train had to stop at Clevedon and be led over the crossing at
4 mph by a flagman. The Act went on to stipulate that rails should weigh at
least 60 lb./yd and check rails were to be provided at curves less than 9
chains radius. In the event of flat-bottomed rail being used, rails at the joints
had to be secured by fang, or other through bolts, or by coach screws or
double spikes on the outside with a bearing plate. On a curve of less than 9
chains, the rails were required to be secured as above and tied to gauge by
iron or steel ties.

Turntables were not required, but no engine was to run tender first at more
than 15 mph, though in the event, this restriction proved unnecessary as the
WCPLR never possessed any tender engines. Home signals were to be
erected at loops and if a home signal could not be sighted from a distance of
a quarter of a mile, a distant signal was required. At the junction with the
GWR at Clevedon, separate home signals for each line were required.

Platforms had to be provided unless the coaches were adapted for ground
level access. Axle loads were not to exceed 12 tons and the maximum speed
restriction was 25 mph with a lower limit of 10 mph at ungated level
crossings and round curves less than 9 chains radius. A capital of £21,000,
with £7000 loans, was empowered to be raised in addition to that authorised
in 1885 and 1892.

In 1903 Edward Wintour returned to Lambeth Waterworks and George S.
Newton (the company's accountant since 1898), was appointed manager in
his place.

The company was in a parlous state financially, its account having been in
the red at opening, never to enter the black. During the first seven months of
operation 84,500 passengers were carried, receipts totalling £1695 giving an
average income of almost 5d. per passenger. The second half of the year
included summer traffic, 138,000 passengers being carried. Profit for the
year was £1084, allowing no dividend on ordinary shares.[1] 1899 saw
slightly increased receipts and expenses giving a lower profit of £772, the
dividend on preference shares being reduced from 4 to 3 per cent. Some of
the increased expenditure arose from the need to provide horse buses at
Weston-super-Mare to feed the rather remote station with traffic. The company was faced with the expense of replacing the unsatisfactory cheap semi-
circular cross-section split unseasoned timber sleepers with those of conventional rectangular pattern.[2] There were bright periods such as August

Bank Holiday 1902 when the WCPLR brought 3000 trippers to Weston-super-Mare[3] while, in an effort to gain more traffic, in December it was announced that from the 1st January, 1903 'rates for first and second class season tickets will be considerably reduced'.[4]

The 8¼ miles of line, plus some works on the Portishead section, had cost £83,877,[5] this figure of £10,000 a mile grossly exceeding the original prospectus's estimate of £3000. By 18th October, 1898 only £30,000 of the authorised capital had been raised and the annual shareholders meeting on that date allowed the creation and issue of 4 per cent preference shares for the balance of £20,000. This suggests that at the time of opening the company was in debt to the tune of some £53,000. By June 1899 £14,570 had been raised by the new preference shares and a further £4000 from ordinary shares, while by December, the company's subscribed capital was £69,234.

On 8th October, 1902 an application was heard in the Chancery Division on behalf of the Sheriff of the City & County of Bristol for a Receiver to be appointed due to the company's failure to pay a £500 debt. A Lloyds' bond was 'found' and the application conditionally withdrawn. By 1904 the company owed £76,000, a very considerable sum in those days.

A new undertaking, the Weston, Clevedon & Portishead Docks Railway Company Limited was registered on 19th October, 1904 to obtain control of the light railway by acquiring the whole of the debenture issue and at least 80 per cent of the paid up share capital of the Weston, Clevedon & Portishead Light Railway Company, to pay off its debts and liabilities, and complete the line to Portishead. The prospectus enthusiastically stated:

> The completed line will have for one of its terminii the docks at Portishead. The railway will give access to an extensive area of dairy farm lands and market gardens. These should give a large outwards traffic of cattle, foodstuffs, etc. considerable quantities of which now go by road, and it will be the policy of the board to encourage farmers by offers of special facilities for their traffic. There are near the line of the railway several large quarries, at present being actively worked for the production of building stone, and also limestone of a special quality used in gasworks and for sugar-refining, the production of which quarries at the present time has to be conveyed for many miles by road traction. The Manager of the existing line reports an offer from the proprietor of one quarry alone of traffic of 500 tons per week as soon as the line has been completed.

The authorised capital of this new company was £120,000; comprising £60,000 in ordinary shares, £30,000 in 5 per cent cumulative preference shares and £30,000 in 5 per cent non-cumulative shares.[6] The new company's Engineer was F. Stileman and its Secretary H. J. Hardy.

John Fell prepared the traffic estimate, it being curious that he should be asked again when his previous estimate for building the line from Clevedon to Weston-super-Mare had proved so inadequate. This time he forecast:

2,100,000 passengers annually at an average fare of 3d.	=	£26,250
150,000 tons of goods at an average of 10d. ton	=	£ 6,250

Total income was estimated at £32,500 and allowing 50 per cent for working expenses, a rent charge of £460 and £1000 for management, Directors' fees etc., predicted a new annual profit of £14,790.

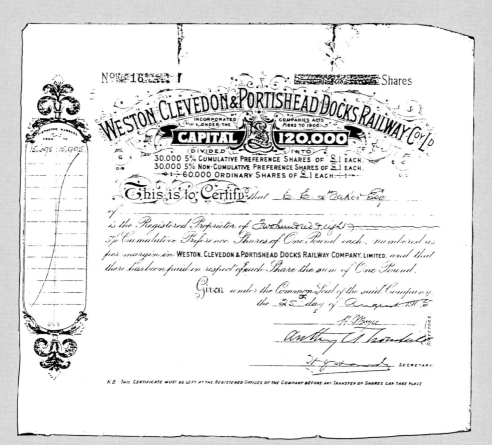

Share Certificate for the new undertaking issued in 1905.

Local passenger timetable for Winter 1898.

Nov. & Dec.]	TIME TABLE.										[1898.		
DOWN				WEEK-DAYS.							SUNDAYS.		
	a.m	a.m	a.m	p.m	p.m	p.m	p.m	p.m	Saturdays only.	p.m p.m p.m	p.m p.m	p.m p.m	p.m
Clevedon dep...	8 15	10 0	11 30	2 15	4 15	7 0	9 0			....	2 15 5	0 8	15
Colehouse Lane ,, ..	8 18	10 3	11 33	2 18	4 18	7 3	9 3			....	2 18 5	3 8	18
Kingston Road ,, ..	8 22	10 7	11 37	2 22	4 22	7 7	9 7			....	2 22 5	7 8	22
Ham Lane ,, ..	8 26	10 11	11 41	2 26	4 26	7 11	9 11			....	2 26 5	11 8	26
Wick St. Lawrence ,, ..	8 30	10 15	11 45	2 30	4 30	7 16	9 16			....	2 30 5	16 8	30
Ebdon Lane ,, ..	8 33	10 18	11 48	2 33	4 33	7 20	9 20			....	2 33 5	20 8	33
Worle ,, ..	8 38	10 23	11 53	2 38	4 38	7 25	9 25			....	2 38 5	25 8	38
Milton Road ,, ..	8 42	10 28	11 58	2 42	4 42	7 30	9 30			....	2 42 5	30 8	43
Weston-s-Mare arr..	8 46	10 32	12 2	2 46	4 46	7 35	9 35			....	2 46 5	35 8	48

UP													
	a.m	a.m	p.m	p.m	p.m	p.m	p.m	Saturdays only.	p.m p.m p.m	p.m p.m p.m			
Weston-s-Mare dep...9	0	10 45	12 15	3 0	5 0	7 45	10 0		....	3 0 5 45	9 0		
Milton Road ,, ...9	3	10 48	12 18	3 3	5 3	7 49	10 4		....	3 3 5 48	9 4		
Worle ,, ...9	8	10 53	12 23	3 8	5 8	7 55	10 10		....	3 8 5 54	9 10		
Ebdon Lane ,, ...9	13	10 57	12 28	3 13	5 13	8 0	10 15		....	3 13 5 59	9 15		
Wick St. Lawrence ,, ...9	17	11 1	12 32	3 17	5 17	8 4	10 19		....	3 17 6 3	9 19		
Ham Lane ,, ...9	21	11 5	12 36	3 21	5 21	8 8	10 23		....	3 21 6 7	9 23		
Kingston Road ,, ...9	26	11 10	12 41	3 26	5 26	8 13	10 28		....	3 26 6 12	9 28		
Colehouse Lane ,, ...9	30	11 13	12 45	3 30	5 30	8 17	10 32		....	3 30 6 16	9 32		
Clevedon arr ...9	34	11 16	12 48	3 34	5 34	8 21	10 36		....	3 34 6 20	9 36		

The Trams will not run on Christmas Day.
The Company's Omnibusses meet all Trains at Weston. See other side for times.
E. R. WINTOUR, Traffic Manager.

A finance organisation, the Leeds Trust Limited, undertook to procure and pay off the debts and liabilities of the WCPLR, and, in consideration of this, the Docks Company guaranteed to pay £70,500 in cash or debentures at par and 90,000 preference shares. The agreement between the Docks Company and Leeds Trust Limited stated that the WCPLR had immediate debts to a total of approximately £30,000 secured on Lloyds Bonds, and that J. F. R. Daniel was jointly responsible for payment of these debts and that a sum of £4145 was due.

The first meeting of the Docks Company was held on 12th January, 1905 at 22–23 Cullum Street, London when it was reported that £21,365 had been received. The Leeds Trust agreed to get Messrs Jackson & Co. to complete the line to Portishead 'on or before 1st July, 1905(!) to the satisfaction of the Board of Trade, for a sum not greater than £22,000'. The Docks Company kept changing its address — late in 1905 it occupied 1 St Mary's Axe; 1906, 14 Ironmonger Lane, London and 1909, 8 Bond Place, Leeds. The Docks Company raised much of the cash for the Portishead extension, though the Docks Company, like the WCPLR itself, was under-subscribed. The Docks Company's 1908 balance sheet showed only £86,758 in shares out of the authorised £120,000, J. F. R. Daniel himself investing over £13,000. However the Docks Company certainly helped the WCPLR to open to Portishead in only three years compared with the twelve necessary for opening Clevedon to Weston-super-Mare. The Docks Company probably never actually took over the Weston, Clevedon & Portishead Company. On 17th May, 1912 a Receiver was appointed to the Docks Company, Herbert Leigh Williams, chartered accountant of 70 Queen Victoria Street, London. In July 1925 C.E. Heath of the Excess Insurance Company* paid the remaining creditors thus clearing the £70,000 debt for £1500, the Receiver being discharged in October 1925 without presenting accounts. The company was dissolved by notice in *The London Gazette* of 26th April, 1929.

Returning to the fortunes of the WCPLR itself, in the summer of 1904 as the five years allowed for building the Portishead extension had almost expired, on 25th July, a fortnight before time ran out, workmen laid rails over the Kenn Road crossing, Clevedon. The company knew that if it did not do so, such powers would not readily be renewed. Other preliminary preparations made around this date were the erection of a workmen's hut and timbers being conveyed to crossings over the rhines. In December a shipload of rails and sleepers arrived at Portishead and by mid-January 1905, two miles of track had been laid.

In 1905 fresh petitions were made for a Receiver to be appointed and controversy broke out anew between the railway and the CUDC. At a meeting of the Council on 20th July, 1905, it was revealed that it had sought counsel of Mr Forbes Lankester, KC. His opinion was that powers under the 1899 Act had ceased on 7th August, 1904 except as far as the railway was then complete. He considered that the council should give the company notice and that the company was no longer entitled to keep its rails in the roadway. 'The council should at the same time give the company notice to remove the rails and notice in default that the council will proceed to remove them themselves'. It was his opinion that if the company failed to

---

*See page 37.

remove the lines within a reasonable time, the council would be in a position to defend itself successfully in any action the company might bring.

With this opinion to back it, the council gave the WCPLR fourteen days notice to remove its rails from the roads. But as might have been expected, the notice expired and the metals were still in place. The general feeling on the council now was that the company should not be prevented from completing its line so long as satisfactory terms regarding the level crossings could be arranged, and it was given seven days' notice to remove the rails, and if by the end of that period it had failed to do so, the CUDC threatened to remove them and charge the expense to the company.

The company's solicitors in their turn wrote to the CUDC saying that it failed to appreciate on what grounds the council based its claim to be entitled to remove the rails. If an explanation was not forthcoming, an injunction would be applied for to restrain the council from carrying into effect its threat. The CUDC's solicitor, M. C. A. Day, replied saying that the council did not wish to act in a hostile spirit, but wished only to protect the public at level crossings, and that perhaps satisfactory terms could be arranged at a meeting. However, the CUDC was still unswerving in its determination to remove the rails and at its meeting on 6th September, Day reported that all the rails had been taken up from the council's roadways before 10.30 am on Tuesday 29th August and at 4.30 pm the same day he had received a telegram from the company's solicitors saying that a writ had been issued against the CUDC and an injunction granted by Justice Lawrence. An ordinary interim injunction was served on the Clerk of the Council.

Day applied for an adjournment to arrange terms, but the plaintiffs would not agree. He was confident that the council would win and the WCPLR have to come in on the CUDC's terms, or go to the expense of applying for a fresh Act. Two members of the council, Messrs Ascott and Jones, had an interview with J. F. R. Daniel, the railway's Secretary. He said he was quite willing to meet the CUDC at any time and arrange terms to stop litigation, going so far as to put his proposals into writing:

> No whistling on approaching or departing near the church — trams to stop dead before crossing.
> Gates across railway to be opened for passing of trams and closed after.
> Trams to cross the road at a walking pace, 4 miles an hour.
> Gateman to walk in front of the engine when crossing a road.
> Roads at crossings to be kept in repair by the company.
> No crossing the Kenn Road at the time of Great Western Railway trains arriving or departing.

Several members of the CUDC expressed the opinion that Ascott and Jones were 'out of order' in interviewing Daniel and the Chairman confirmed that in view of the resolution of the council, they were indeed 'out of order'.

On 29th September, a sub-committee recommended that all level crossings should be gated to cover both the road and the railway and legal cost of the dispute should be paid by the WCPLR. The railway agreed to provide gates, subject to certain engineering modifications, but believed that each party should pay its own legal costs. Later the WCPLR offered 25 guineas for the expense of the Agreement which would be drawn up. On 19th October the CUDC accepted the proposal and the Agreement was at last signed in November.

Rails were reinstated on the Kenn Road Crossing during the first week of January 1905 and on the 10th a train ran over it with the locomotive whistling and detonators exploding. On 26th January a trial trip was made between Clevedon and the outskirts of Portishead carrying G. S. Newton, traffic manager, guard H. Davey, conductor W. Whiting, driver J. Jones and several permanent way men. The *Clevedon Mercury* reported that:

> . . . the line runs through a district hitherto unknown to tourists and full of interest, while it is also the only direct and cheapest route between the three watering-places of Clevedon, Portishead, and Weston, each of which has its peculiar charms. One is sylvan, the other quiet and pretty, and they all have invigorating breezes from the Atlantic full of ozone.

Attention was then concentrated on bridging two rhines on the fringe of Portishead, though this involved no serious engineering difficulties. The line was fenced with post and wire, the top and middle strands being barbed. In the last week of July, Messrs Saxby & Farmer were fixing the signalling apparatus for the East Clevedon gates, the same firm also supplying Kenn Road gates near the GWR station. Tickets for the various stations were now being printed.

Col R. G. von Donop was inspecting officer for the visit on 31st July making this report:[7]

> 1st August 1907
>
> SIR, I have the honour to report for the information of the Board of Trade, that in compliance with the instruction contained in your Minute of the 22nd instant, I have inspected a portion of the Weston-super-Mare, Clevedon, & Portishead Light Railway, which has been constructed by the Co. under their Act of 1899.
>
> The portion of line under inspection is that lying between Clevedon and Portishead, forming Light Railway No. 1 of the above-named Act.
>
> The new line commences at Clevedon Station by an end-on junction with the existing portion of the railway, and terminated at Portishead Station, a distance of 5m. 67chs. The line is single throughout, without passing places.
>
> The gauge of the line is 4ft 8½in., and the rails consist of flat bottomed rails, 30 ft in length, weighing 60 lb. to the yard. The sleepers are 9 ft by 9 in. by 4½ in., their distance from centre to centre being 3 ft, except at the rail joints, where they are 2ft 4½in. apart. The rails are secured together by fish-plates, and each rail is fixed to the sleepers by spikes and six fang bolts. The ballast consists of broken stone, said to be laid to a depth of 9 in. below the surface. The fencing is of posts and wires. No special difficulty has been met with in connection with the drainage.
>
> The steepest gradient on the line is 1 in 68, extending for a length of 15 chs; the sharpest curve is of 16 chs radius.
>
> There are no cuttings or embankments calling for mention.
>
> There are 5 underbridges, varying in span from 6 ft to 34 ft; 4 of them consist of steel girders resting on stone abutments, and the 5th is of timber. There are no viaducts or tunnels. The bridges have sufficient theoretical strength for an axle load of 8 tons which is the minimum axle load to be made use of, and they proved themselves stiff under test.

Gates closing across the railway have been erected at roads marked 26, 38 & 42 in the Parish of Clevedon and at roads marked 3 in the Parish of Portishead, also at Parnell Road, Clevedon. (Road 21 in Parish of Portishead is not on Rly No. 1). At all other public road crossings cattle guards are constructed.

There are the following stations or halts on the line:

(1) East Clevedon	–	platform on ground level	
(2) Walton Park	–	do	with small shelter and a siding
(3) Walton in Gordano		do	
Cadbury Lane [sic]		do	
Portishead South		do	and a siding

Portishead – platform on ground level with waiting room and booking office; an engine-run-round road is provided, but as it is not trapped it must not be used as a siding; to this the Co. agrees; there is also a siding connection.

The line is to be worked by one Engine in steam carrying a staff, and the Co. should be asked to give an undertaking to this effect.

There are no signals on the line, all the points leading to sidings being locked by a key on the staff.

The following improvements are noted which the Co. has agreed to carry out forthwith:

(1) The key locking the siding connection should be an integral part of the staff instead of being rudely attached to it by a chain.

(2) An additional grid required at one cattle guard as pointed out.

(3) Cattle guards to be provided at one side of Lower Queen's Road, Clevedon.

(4) Gates across the Railway to be provided at Road No. 10 in the Parish of Clevedon. The Co. informed me that the reason of these not having been already provided was on account of delay in arriving at an understanding with the local Authorities as to exactly what should be done. An agreement had now been arrived at and the work would be put in hand at once. Meanwhile speed over this road would not exceed four miles an hour and a man should be stationed at the road (Ken Rd) [sic] while a train is passing.

The line appears to be substantially constructed and subject to the fulfillment of the above mentioned requirements, the completion of which should be reported in due course I can recommend the Board of Trade to sanction the line being brought into use.

I have etc.,
P. G. von Donop

(The Company is anxious to open on Wednesday the 7th and there is no objection to their doing so. They would therefore be glad to receive the certificate at once.)

On 7th August the first train ran without ceremony, two trains leaving Clevedon to Weston and Portishead at 8.05 and 8.10 am respectively, the latter appropriately enough hauled by the Manning Wardle saddle tank *Portishead*, with the Engineer Francis Stileman and traffic manager George Newton on board. On their return journeys the well filled trains ran from terminus to terminus, detonators exploding at the end of each run.

The *Clevedon Mercury*[8] carried the column:

THE LIGHT RAILWAY TO PORTISHEAD
OPENING ON WEDNESDAY
The extension of the Weston, Clevedon, and Portishead Light Railway to the latter seaside resort became an accomplished fact on Wednesday, when without any ceremony the first passenger trains were run, they beginning a service between the two towns which is bound to become increasingly appreciated as time goes on. The extension also offers a valuable link with Weston-super-Mare, and the convenient trains arranged do not seem to be wanting in patronage, though possibly some have gone for the novelty of the ride or because they have been holiday keeping. Clevedon and Portishead have much in common, both places relying largely on visitors for their prosperity, and the comfortable and easy travelling provided by the company, under the superintendence of Mr G. S. Newton (traffic manager) should do much to promote the welfare of the two towns. The trains each way are numerous, and the ride between Clevedon and Portishead is a remarkably pretty one in point of scenery, running as it does through the celebrated Nightingale Valley. It has taken longer to complete the undertaking than expected. As far back as Easter the scheme was so far advanced that from the out-skirts of Portishead trains travelled to Clevedon and back. Attention was then given to the heaviest bit of work in the undertaking, viz, the bridging of two rhines on the fringe of Portishead. This involved no serious engineering difficulty, indeed, the scheme throughout in this particular has been a very simple one. Here and there the line passes through a shallow cutting, but for the most part its course is over nearly flat land above which it is raised by an embankment a few feet in height. At Portishead the terminus is about half a mile from the Great Western Railway station. It is close to the main road, and most conveniently situated for residents. There are no platforms, but road gravel walks suffice for passengers, while for the station a picturesque little rustic building of wood does duty. The track is of standard gauge, and is double at the Portishead end. The journey to Clevedon including stoppages at intervening stations, takes about half-an-hour, and it is expected this section of the line will be the means of tapping a considerable goods traffic, as well as passengers. The new coaches resemble those on the Midland line on the exterior, while the interior is in the Pulman [sic] style, and is tastefully decorated. Leaving Clevedon, the route is across meadows through the pleasant valley bounded on the one side by the line of hills on which are Failand and Cadbury Camp, and on the other by the ridge dividing the vale from the sea. The scenery is picturesque, and where the valley narrows, it is strikingly beautiful. The trip over the line is a pleasant one, and the stopping places will open up new possibilities to those fond of country rambles. On the through journey from Portishead to Weston-super-Mare passengers go through Portbury and Bristol Road, Clapton Road, Weston-in-Gordano (a village possessing a church with considerable archaeological interest), Walton-in-Gordano, and East Clevedon. After passing through the present light railway station at Clevedon, the railway has stopping places at Colehouse Lane, Kingston Road, Ham Lane, Wick St. Lawrence, Ebdon Lane, Worle, and Milton Road, and terminates in Ashcombe Road, Weston-super-Mare. Besides Portishead, Clevedon, and Weston, the railway, therefore, gives tourists and villagers an opportunity of joining or leaving the train at a dozen intermediate points.

A leader in the *Clevedon Mercury*[9] read:

The crossing at East Clevedon had been talked about and its working has been watched. The gates are guarded by a man who opens and shuts them by means of levers, and there seems no possibility of accident, as even those who were at first opposed to them have been ready to admit.

This same leader praised the extension for its convenience, frequent service and low cost of travel.

To cover carriage stock requirements, seven four-wheeled coaches made redundant by the Metropolitan Railway electrification were received, no doubt very cheaply and were first used on 2nd September. On Wednesdays (early closing day) cheap excursions were run from Clevedon to Portishead, or Clevedon to Weston, at the return fare of 6d. and were well patronised. Every Thursday (early closing at Portishead) an excursion was run from Portishead to Weston at the fare of 1s. for the 28 mile return journey.

On 11th May, 1908 the WCPLR sent a letter to the Board of Trade stating that while under Section 32 of the Act, sub-section 2, an axle load of 12 tons was permitted, the inspector only allowed an axle load of 8 tons, less than that borne by any of the company's engines[10] and less than sufficient to enable a locomotive to haul a loaded train over gradients of the new extension which included a stretch of 1 in 68. The Board replied saying that it had no objection to raising the limit to 12 tons.

The first exchange with the GWR at Portishead was not made until 2nd November, 1908, the *Clevedon Mercury*[11] again commenting:

THE LIGHT RAILWAY
IMPROVED GOODS TRAFFIC FACILITIES
   Considerable local interest is aroused by the fact that the Light Railway has now been connected with the GWR at Portishead, this opening up the probability of a great extension of goods traffic over the former line. The first train passed over the new junction on Monday, the connection having been made by the GWR, the works being on a scale calculated for the interchange of a large amount of goods traffic, comprising nearly 1,000 yards of junction lines and sidings, with cross-over roads and other facilities, and a new sea-wall a quarter of a mile in length, of considerable thickness, and covered with puddled clay. Goods can now be consigned via the Light Railway to Clevedon, Weston-super-Mare and other stations, by which not only will an economy in cost be effected, but what is often more important, the delivery of the same will be expedited, an advantage business men will not be slow to note. It is certain the new route will be largely used, and the Light Railway authorities are to be congratulated upon having secured the connection.

The new sea wall failed to protect the station against a violent storm which occurred in December 1910 when the station and its approaches were flooded and impassable.

Colonel von Donop inspected and passed some new works on 5th January, 1909. A new run-round siding had been opened at Weston on the west side of the running line; home signals erected at each end of Clevedon station, signals and siding points being worked from a ground frame of two levers.[12]

In the Railway Rates and Charges Order Confirmation Act of 16th August, 1909 (9 Edw. 7 cap. 92) under the Railway and Canal Traffic Act of 1888, the classification of merchandise and maximum rates and charges on the WCPLR were made those of the GWR Order Confirmation Act of 1891.

An interesting proposal was put forward in November 1912 when the Great Western Directors considered building a new station at the bottom of

Nore Road, where the Western Region erected a new station in 1954, it being planned to accommodate the WCPLR to facilitate interchange. This imaginative plan proved abortive.

Notes:

1. *Clevedon Mercury*, 22nd October, 1898
2. *Ibid*, 23rd June, 1900
3. *Weston Mercury*, 9th August, 1902
4. *Ibid*, 20th December, 1902
5. *Clevedon Mercury*, 22nd October, 1898
6. *Bradshaw's Railway Manual, Shareholders' Guide & Directory*, 1908
7. PRO MT6/2484/5
8. *Clevedon Mercury*, 10th August, 1907
9. *Ibid*, 17th August, 1907
10. An untrue statement
11. *Clevedon Mercury*, 7th November, 1908
12. PRO MT6/2163/5

A further posed photograph of *Weston* on a Clevedon to Weston train seen here on the Wick St Lawrence Bridge in August 1899. Note dip in bridge at its far end where the support post was already sinking.   *Locomotive Publishing Co.*

Chapter Five

Into Receivership

Before proceeding further with the line's chronological history, it is necessary to have a further look at the company's finances.

By the spring of 1905, Jackson, contractor for the Weston-super-Mare section had yet to be paid in full; the Avonside Engine Company, Bristol was owed money for locomotive repairs and there were various other creditors. On 20th June, 1905 debenture holders authorised the borrowing of £14,500 from the Excess Insurance Company to complete the Portishead extension, this loan being made on 17th August with 5 per cent mortgage debentures, the capital due for repayment on 1st January, 1907. By June 1906 the WCPLR was again short of funds, but managed to borrow nearly £16,000 from two city merchants. Still needing cash, on 28th March, 1907 an agreement was signed with Cuthbert Eden Heath, Managing Director of the Excess Insurance Company for further sums up to £15,000 on condition that the WCPLR Directors resigned and were replaced by two chosen by Heath. These were his cousin, Spencer Gore-Browne, chief accountant of the Great Indian Peninsular Railway and Chairman of the Cleobury Mortimer & Ditton Priors Light Railway, and Henry I. Coburn. Both had inspected the line the previous December and reported that at Weston-super-Mare a new station, goods accommodation and sidings were necessary, and repairs needed to the Clevedon to Weston section.

By December 1907 the company's capital totalled £114,510, made up of £74,010 in ordinary shares; £20,000 in 4 per cent first preference shares; £6000 in 4½ per cent second preference shares and £14,500 in 5 per cent registered debentures. Heath had bought large parcels of shares, some from the former Chairman Samuel Edward Baker, until at least £63,720, or 56 per cent of the railway's capital was owned by the Excess Insurance Company.

In 1908 receipts totalled £4021, an increase of £1094 over those of 1906, the last full year before the Portishead extension opened. In addition to the Portishead extension causing the deficit in the Capital Account to increase, receipts declined after 1908, while passenger figures peaked as early as 1899 at 242,287. The Docks Company issued an unaudited account in 1908 showing that the WCPLR's liabilities to creditors was £92,948 8s. 10d., plant and equipment were valued at £165,000, while cash in hand totalled only 1s. 11d.! Cost of constructing the line from Portishead to Weston-super-Mare was £76,468 16s. 11d., proving Fell's estimate of £37,000 plus land quite inadequate.

An application in the Chancery Division on 2nd July, 1913 to settle the order of priorities of the creditors resulted in the 1904 company, the Weston, Clevedon & Portishead Docks & Railway Company Limited claiming a debt of £76,656 17s. 9d. from the statutory company, which was now admitted at £70,000 without interest and placed last in order of priority.[1]

It is believed that Heath took over the line hoping that the GWR would make an attractive offer. Income for the year following the opening of the Portishead section was less than expenditure, because early in 1909 Heath bought out other creditors and petitioned for Gore-Browne to be appointed Receiver and Manager, citing a debt of £893, plus interest. This order was granted by Mr Justice Joyce in the Chancery Division hearing and confirmed in *The London Gazette* 30th July, 1909. Thus the Excess Insurance Company became the proprietor of the WCPLR and the Directors ceased to have any powers regarding the running of the line.[2] Although the WCPLR was more fortunate than most light railways in being connected to no less than four industrial concerns — two gas works and two quarries, the company's main trouble was that its debts were too large to be paid off.

Notes:

1. *Clevedon Mercury*, 5th July, 1913
2. Acknowledgement is due to Christopher Redwood, *The Weston, Clevedon & Portishead Railway*, Sequoia Publishing, 1981 for bringing to light much of the financial information.

The Light Railway's horse bus (*c.*1900) which ran between Weston-super-Mare station and the Old Pier.   *Colonel Stephens' Railway Museum*

Chapter Six
Proposed extensions

The WCPLR still hankered after direct access to the sea front at Weston-super-Mare as this they felt would have improved its traffic. Two schemes were put forward: either the Weston-super-Mare & District Electric Supply Company Limited's electric tramway could be extended 25 chains from Locking Road along Ashcombe Road to the Light Railway terminus at a cost of £2500, or a link built from an end-on junction with the Locking Road tramway to join the WCPLR near Milton Road station at a cost of £4445. The latter was anticipated to generate annual income of £520 from passenger and £56 from mineral traffic, working expenses being £183. Stephen Sellon, Consulting Engineer to the promoters and former Engineer to Weston-super-Mare electric tramways, preferred the latter scheme and said that if the entire WCPLR was converted to electric traction, an annual saving of £2800 would be made in running costs. No details were given, but it is presumed that an electric tram would have hauled a WCPLR car along the street tramway. Being in Receivership, the WCPLR was unable to raise cash for new works, so in 1910 an independent company was set up. An inquiry was held at the Grand Atlantic Hotel, Weston-super-Mare on 26th February, 1910[1] before Light Railway Commissioners Col G. F. O. Boughey and H. A. Steward. The line was supported by both paddle steamer operators using the pier, Messrs P. & A. Campbell Ltd and the Red Funnel Fleet; a Light Railway Order was granted on 12th November, 1910.

The authorised capital was £9000 in £1 shares with borrowing powers of £3000. Land was actually bought and fenced off, but no further steps were taken and the project proved abortive. In 1913 interviews took place between the Weston-super-Mare & District Electric Supply Company and Col H. F. Stephens of the WCPLR. The former offered to operate the Junction line for a payment of 4d. per single journey, this figure to include provision of cars, drivers, current, conductors and tickets, but exclusive of maintenance of permanent way and overhead equipment. Even if the scheme had come to fruition, it is doubtful whether the extra traffic generated would have made a significant difference to the WCPLR income, as the type of person who favoured Weston-super-Mare was unlikely to enjoy the select watering place of Clevedon, or vice versa.*

At the Light Railway Order inquiry H. H. Matthews, Secretary of the WCPLR from 1907 to 1911, revealed that at one time he envisaged extending the WCPLR 12 miles to Edington Junction on the Somerset & Dorset Joint Railway. The GWR's Bristol district superintendent visited the WCPLR early in 1912 and revealed in a report[2] that at one time the GWR would have been interested in buying it to prevent the S&DJR extending from Edington Junction to Weston-super-Mare, or making an 8 mile long branch from Burnham-on-Sea to Weston. This latter proposal was resurrected in June 1918. Although the Weston-super-Mare & District Electric Supply Company decided not to take any financial interest in the scheme (which proved abortive) it offered to give any facilities required.

When a proposal was made to re-open a coalpit near Clapton Court in the Gordano Valley, the Cadbury Light Railway Company was planned to form a

(*For further details of the electric tramway see *Weston-super-Mare Tramways* by C. Maggs, Oakwood Press, Locomotion Papers No. 78.)

connection 1½ miles long between the mine and the WCPLR. H. F. Stephens was Engineer and Cuthbert Eden Heath of the Excess Insurance Company, the first Director. With a proposed capital of £9000 and estimated cost of £8873 very little would have been available to meet any contingencies. A triangular junction near Black Rock Quarry sidings would have allowed through running to either Portishead or Clevedon. The plan was scotched by the objections of Clevedon Rural District Council to road crossings.

Notes:

1. *Weston Mercury,* 5th March, 1910
2. PRO: RAIL 253/532

The newly acquired locomotive *Hesperus* still bearings its GWR brass number of 1384, seen here at Portishead in 1911. Conductor Bill Cullen has a Williamson ticket punch; his cap bears the initials 'WC&PR'.   *Author's Collection*

A further static view of a gleaming *Weston* at Weston-super-Mare in July 1899.
Driver George Hancock stands proudly by his locomotive with the conductor on
the car verandah. Note the round porthole in the sliding door above his left shoulder.
This locomotive, being the first named *Weston*, came from the Furness Railway in
June 1899 (No. 35). It was a 2−2−2 well tank built by Sharp Stewart in 1864. As it
was more powerful than *Clevedon*, it was not scrapped until 1906.

P. Strange Collection

A period photograph of the 2−4−0 locomotive *Hesperus* at Portishead in April 1911.
Note the plate to widen the front of the cab to provide more crew protection as
compared with the photograph opposite.   *J.J. Herd Collection*

Conductor Bill Cullen with other staff c.1909.
Author's Collection

A close-up view at Weston-super-Mare in 1909. Notice the uncoupled vacuum brake pipes; also the safety chains; bogie restraining chains; the high step when boarding from ground level and the low platform beyond.
Author's Collection

Chapter Seven
1911 until Closure

When Major H. F. Stephens was appointed manager in 1911 he sent a deputy, E. Smith, to Clevedon to supervise temporarily until A. J. Grundy, who had been with Stephens on the Kent & East Sussex Railway, was appointed local manager at Clevedon. Stephens, operating from Tonbridge proved impractical, the distance leading to expensive telephone bills the company could ill afford. Stephens also ordered tickets by the ten thousand in order to receive a discount for quantity and some stocks had hardly been touched when the line closed in 1940! He would have purchased the Bideford, Westward Ho! & Appledore Railway's bogie coaches when that concern closed on 28th March, 1917 had not the track been removed leaving them stranded high and dry in the shed.[1]

Around the end of 1911 another attempt was made to persuade the GWR to purchase the line, and the GWR's Bristol district superintendent and divisional engineer both visited the line, the former writing a report.[2]

GREAT WESTERN RAILWAY
BRISTOL

Gentlemen,   *February 20th 1912.*

Weston-s-Mare, Clevedon and Portishead Light Railway

We have thought it necessary in considering the proposal submitted by Mr J. F. R. Daniel, that this Company should undertake the working of the Light Railway between Portishead and Weston-s-Mare to make a quiet and superficial inspection of the Line and with this object in view we travelled over the line as passengers, the Divisional Engineer accompanying us.

The attached will give a general idea of the equipment of the Line and we are agreed that if it were seriously contemplated to take over the working, a considerable sum would have to be expended in bringing the condition of the line up to anything approaching the standard condition of our own property as we consider that with the present arrangements in connection with the public level crossings and at the haltes, of which there is a considerable number, the Company would be exposed to some risk in working, which they would not be justified in incurring.

The Line throughout is crossed a great many times by accommodation crossings as will be seen by the list attached hereto.

We cannot offer an opinion as to the condition of the stock owned by or what is represented as the stock belonging to the Light Railway Company but we note that this item is covered by the proposal to submit such stock to valuation.

We have no particulars of the Staff employed on the Light Railway but from observations we feel that an improvement in this direction would have to be adopted both in quality of employee and probably in point of numbers and as a certainty the staff who would be employed would have to be enrolled as Great Western staff, pure and simple, and would therefore come within the conditions of service appertaining to same.

We have nothing to guide us as to the actual earnings of the Line but from information gathered from one source and another and from observations we can only come to the conclusion that this Company could not work the Line at a profit and it would be interesting to have an opportunity of criticising any statement of accounts prepared by the Light Railway Company.

We have reported upon this undertaking from time to time and as will be seen from our reports, we were at one time in favour of this Company acquiring the property at a low figure, for one particular reason, viz:- to prevent any competing Company, whose interests are within easy distance of the Weston, Clevedon and Portishead Light Railway, acquiring control.

This view was repeated on the occasion of the journey made by the late General Manager and other chief officers in May 1909 but we believe it was then definitely decided that it would not be to the interests of the Company to acquire the property.

Since that date the compact between the South Western Company and ourselves has come into existence and as that Company are part owners of the Somerset and Dorset Line, there are not in our opinion such strong grounds for the purchase of the Line.

If acquired by this Company the Line could not be profitably adopted for any through working and the local traffic that would accrue to us by working on the same lines as now exist, would to a considerable extent be competing with our system as between Portishead, Clevedon and Weston-super-Mare.

If the proposal by Mr Daniel that this Company should work the Line were for one moment entertained it should be on condition that it should first be put in such order as to ensure absolute safe working and that the payment to this Company should be on a basis that would secure to us the actual cost for maintaining and working as a minimum, and a share in the profits if any accrued but of this we have serious doubts, as to whether the Line could be so developed as to show any balance on the credit side of the account.

We cannot see that the Company would in any way gain by taking over the working of the Railway and accordingly recommend the proposal being declined.

During World War I two halts were opened: Clevedon All Saints' (October 1917) and Broadstone (August 1918) so that there were now stops at almost every place where the railway crossed a road. In 1917 a siding was put in to serve the Munition Box Works, later, Shoplands, just east of Parnell Road. In 1914 a special troop train was run to carry the Clevedon Detachment of the Wessex Royal Engineers from Clevedon to Weston-super-Mare, while later in the War a large number of other troops were billeted in houses along the Gordano Valley and when they received orders to move to France, a special train was run to carry them to Clevedon where the regiment reformed.[3] During the War it was alleged that brass number and nameplates were removed from the locomotives in the drive to collect scrap metal for the war effort. This was apparently untrue. The large brass nameplates were certainly removed from the Dübs 2−4−0T *Clevedon*, but one of these is now in the possession of the Bristol Railway Circle, while the location of the other is unknown. The oval plates bearing the name *Weston* were still in the offices at Clevedon in 1938[4] and probably exist today in a private collection.

On 27th September, 1919 the permanent way staff joined the national strike, traffic being halted two days later when the remaining union members withdrew their labour. A skeleton service was resumed on 1st October.

The Bristol Tramways & Carriage Company arrived at Clevedon with a bus service from Bristol in May 1920. The following year real competition with the WCPLR began with three buses from Clevedon to Portishead operated daily, including Sundays when there were no Light Railway trains on this section. In 1927 a bus service from Clevedon to Weston-super-Mare was inaugurated.

As most of the employees were not trade union members, the 1926 General Strike had little effect on the WCPLR, the two men participating being dismissed. Stephens lent two footplate crews[5] to the GWR's shed at Bath Road, Bristol, and the GWR requested the loan of the Drewry railcar and trailer to operate peak hour services on its Yatton to Clevedon branch, but in the event they were not needed.

Mineral traffic was important, the Light Railway carrying about 80,000 tons annually, a large proportion emanating from the line's principal trader, Black Rock Quarries. In 1931 that company, having installed new plant which it hoped would greatly increase its output, gave land to the WCPLR to lay extra sidings which were finished in October that year at a cost of £300 to the railway. Unfortunately, far from increasing, output from the quarry declined. This was because shortly after the sidings had been laid, Black Rock Quarries were taken over by Bryant & Langford Quarries Limited and, three years later, Roads Reconstruction (1934) Limited was formed. As Black Rock was now under the same ownership as quarries connected directly to the GWR, it made economic sense to divert railway ballast orders to these other quarries, thus avoiding the extra sixpence per ton carriage charge over the WCPLR. Black Rock was then chiefly used for orders removed by road. Mineral traffic on the WCPLR in the second half of 1935 shrank to half of what it had been in the first six months.

In 1934 after 13 years service the Drewry railcar needed heavy overhaul and while this was being undertaken she was replaced by a larger Drewry railcar, the former SR No. 5 which had been working the Fareham to Gosport line.

In 1936, the traffic manager W. H. Austen wishing to economise by closing the Clevedon repair shop, sought to hire a locomotive from the GWR, but this was refused, the GWR probably considering it a bad advertisement for one of its engines to be seen on such a ramshackle line. On the other hand it may not have had available a suitable locomotive with a sufficiently light axle load. Austen's solution was to purchase another 'Terrier' from the SR. As the Chancery Master only allowed £405 for its purchase, the balance of £395 was covered by 'repairs'.

Heath's successor at the Excess Insurance Company, E. Merrick Tylor, had a very caring attitude, as is shown in a letter to Austen on 24th August, 1938 when he wrote 'I am endeavouring in every possible way to keep this line open for the benefit of the employees'. His offer to the GWR to carry ballast from Black Rock Quarry for threepence a ton was refused, the GWR's only offer to help being that its general manager Sir James Milne tried to persuade Bristol Corporation which was taking some 40,000 tons of stone from the quarry by road, to use rail. His efforts proved unsuccessful and rail tonnage from Black Rock fell from 34,755 in 1937 to 27,937 in 1938. Helping offset this loss, corresponding figures for the Conygar Pennant Quarry near Walton Park station increased from 3968 to 7940 tons in the same period. On 18th January, 1939 Austen reported that in the previous three months there had been practically no traffic from Black Rock and that if this state of things continued, he could not work the line. By now the Excess Insurance Company had realised it could not recover its claims from the WCPLR, yet closing the line was not a simple matter, requiring an Act of Parliament at a cost of approximately £750.

With the outbreak of World War II, the Ministry of Transport took over control of the main line railways by the Railway Control Order of 1st September, 1939, but the WCPLR was not included. Although railcar operation had undoubtedly led to savings, there were several factors against retaining the line. Passenger traffic was largely seasonal, since few local people were now using it, and the day-tripper traffic from Weston was confined to a few months. The rolling stock was now forty years old, and in some cases, fifty and as roads grew busier, the many level crossings became a heavier responsibility. A Court Order was made for the Receiver to cease operation within four months of 18th March, 1940. H. E. Fulford the Receiver, a barrister who had succeeded Mr Gore-Browne the original Receiver, wrote to the Clerk of Somerset County Council, Taunton, on 1st April, 1947: 'Early in the war after consulting with the Ministry of Transport I closed the line to traffic, and shortly afterwards handed it over, again after consulting with the Ministry, to the Great Western Railway. I then closed my accounts and the proceedings under section 4 of the Railway Companies Act of 1867 were terminated'. In these circumstances the Receiver would normally have returned the line to the railway company, but there was no office, seal, officers, or register of books. The company only existed in name. Following the withdrawal of the Receiver, nobody had the legal right to work the line.

On 15th April Austen wrote to local traders who used the railway to inform them that all traffic would cease on and after Saturday 18th May. The staff was not too distressed as to ease redundancy, wages were paid until the end of September, and, it being wartime, there were no problems finding alternative employment. Some of the staff believed that the reason the WCPLR closed was that Austen hoped that the Army would be interested in taking over the line for training the railway section of the Royal Engineers. Had this happened, it would have been put into good working order at Government expense as was the Shropshire & Montgomeryshire Railway the following year.

Passenger traffic on the last Friday and Saturday was exceptionally heavy, scores of people taking the opportunity of a farewell trip through the charming country which the line had leisurely served.[6] The train for the last trips consisted of coaches Nos. 2 and 4 hauled by locomotive No. 4 which left Clevedon at 4 pm, with three wagons at the rear. On arrival at Portishead, these were pushed to the transfer siding and the train left again at 4.45. Groups gathered at the lineside to wave farewell and a wreath was hung on the smokebox. The train was greeted at Weston-super-Mare by a crowd of over 200. Three policemen were on duty to protect the railway from souvenir hunters. (These precautions were taken because not long before, when electric trams stopped running on one of the Bristol routes, the last car was raided, the controller handle stolen and the driver forced to make his way to the depot with the aid of a spanner.) Weston was left at 6.15 pm to the accompaniment of wild cheering, exploding detonators, whistle-blowing and flag waving. The two coaches were crowded, many people standing on the observation platforms. Two milk churns were dropped off at Ham Lane and, just beyond, the train was held up by two stray sheep on the line. It was suggested that the grass on the railway was more succulent than that in the field.

The death at Clevedon was peaceful. The platform was thronged, but there was no cheering. The coaches were shunted into a siding and the engine fire raked out. The management turned a blind eye as tickets, handbills and other objects were collected as souvenirs. Except for a few wagons in sidings between Clevedon and Weston, all the rest were at Clevedon.

The urban district councils protested at the closure, Clevedon petitioning the Minister of Transport to keep the WCPLR services going until after the war. The Clevedon Gas Company relied upon the line for its substantial coal supplies and for the outward and inward carriage of tar, coke, by-products, appliances and fittings. They believed that closure would have been serious enough under ordinary conditions, but in wartime it threatened to prejudice severely the maintenance of the public gas supply. But the Minister re-mained adamant and refused to intervene as he considered the closing would not gravely impair the district's transport facilities. The gas company was forced to use the GWR with the inconvenience of transhipping the coal from rail to road for the brief haul to the works.

The GWR was asked to take over the WCPLR, but claimed that it would cost £30,000 to bring the track up to its standard for a minor country branch line and such an outlay would be uneconomic. However, following the invasion of France in May 1940 and the ensuing evacuation of Dunkirk, the sudden cessation of coal exports to France jammed South Wales docks and collieries with loaded wagons. The Ministry of Transport approved storage accommodation on the WCPLR and the GWR bought the system from the Excess Insurance Company for £10,000. It became the nominal owners of the railway on 22nd June, 1940, having bought the assets and interests of the Insurance Company, including the right to take possession of the line from the Receiver, but did not inherit the obligation to run a train service.

The Excess Insurance Company never held any title deeds of land belong-ing to the light railway. It held deeds of land it had itself bought adjacent to the line and these deeds were delivered to the GWR. The title deeds and other papers were passed to the GWR solicitor who had Fulford's authority to take what he wanted before the papers were used for salvage to help the war effort. The WCPLR stock registers, account books and other records had been missing for years.

On 16th July, 1940 GWR officials arrived at Clevedon to test the bridge over the River Yeo. They waited for locomotive No. 4 to return from Clapton where it had gone to collect some wagons to provide weight for testing the bridge. It was only able to haul six, as the GWR men were not able to handle the 'Terriers' like WCPLR crews. On arrival at Clevedon a coach was attached to the front and pushed to the bridge. Tall grass covered the track causing the wheels to slip. No sand was available to drop on the line, so the ingenious fireman used a material he had at hand — small coal. This worked and gave the wheels the necessary adhesion but the engine had to stop three times just to raise steam. At last the engineers reached the bridge and calculated that six wagons could be taken over at a time. In actual fact, the GWR stored very few wagons of coal on the WCPLR, these being placed at the Weston end, but later removed in case war damage to the Yeo bridge isolated them. One of the GWR coal trains was sighted with an Oxley Sidings brake van.

All WCPLR locomotives and rolling stock passed into the hands of the GWR. When services ceased the railway possessed five tank engines, a rail tractor, two petrol railcars with four-wheel trailer car, three eight-wheel coaches, eleven four-wheel coaches, twenty-seven open wagons, a box van, carriage truck, machinery wagon and goods brake van. On 21st August, 1940 the GWR gathered all movable WCPLR rolling stock — the coaches, Railcar No. 5, nine wagons and the ex-MR brake van (unused for 16 years) into a train which was drawn slowly by a GWR engine to Swindon via Badminton, for scrapping. All coach steps had to be removed to prevent the main line platforms from being fouled. The small railcar and its trailer travelled on four-wheel well wagons. The ex-GER milk van and 7 ft wheelbase open wagons were broken up at Clevedon being quite unfit to travel. Locomotive No. 4 travelled to Swindon under her own steam, while No. 2 *Portishead* under heavy repair had her wheels replaced, was made safe to travel and taken to Swindon 'dead on the van' together with a wagon load of spares, *Clevedon* also travelling on the 5.50 am ex-Bristol East Depot on a separate occasion.

A visitor to the line in the summer of 1942[7] observed that the line was in a good state of repair and the flangeways at the level crossings had been cleaned out. Weston-super-Mare station was in order and part of the goods yard occupied by an air raid shelter. The station at Portishead was also in good condition and most of the intermediate halts still standing. However, at Clevedon the sheds were falling to pieces and all the rolling stock had gone, except for four hand-worked permanent way trolleys.

Track lifting operations started at Weston on 3rd October, 1942, the removal of track and station buildings from Weston-super-Mare to Ebdon Lane was carried out from this date until the end of the month. The track was cut into 6 to 8 ft lengths, GWR locomotive No. 6 (ex-WCPLR No. 4) and six flat trucks used for its removal. No further work was carried out until the end of February 1943 when commencing at Clevedon, track and station buildings, (with the exception of the latter at Clevedon), were removed as far as the bridge at Wick St Lawrence and Portishead station, work terminating approximately at the beginning of June 1943. Removal had to be by road as the Ministry of Works had ordered locomotive No. 6 to Nottingham, leaving No. 5 (which was useless as the WCPLR water tanks were no longer operational and No. 5 was not fitted with a pump to draw water from rhines, unlike No. 6). The GWR was unable to replace it with another engine as these 'Terriers' were the only locomotives in stock with a maximum axle load of 10 tons. The track from Wick St Lawrence bridge to Ebdon Lane was left *in situ* and removed later.[8] The line yielded about 16,000 tons of metal and 15,000 timber sleepers. Waiting shelters at East Clevedon and Walton-in-Gordano were sold for £3 and made excellent sheds. The former WCPLR offices in Lower Queen's Road, Clevedon were used for storing GWR stationery which was brought in a 'Siphon' and had been left in the GWR coal siding for unloading, it being a very unusual sight to see a van on this road.

The trackbed of the WCPLR lay deserted and neighbouring landowners were not slow in staking their claim. They believed that if they could squat for twelve years, the land would become legally theirs. Hen houses and pig sties were erected to the annoyance of people living nearby. On 10th October, 1945 representatives of the local authorities met to obtain opinions on:

(a) The legal position of the company as it existed
(b) The proper steps to take to acquire possession of the track
(c) The most effective way of dealing with derelict property
(d) How to deal with squatters.

The local councils decided to take over all or most of the land within their areas. This land was still vested in the statutory company, which had ceased to exist and (as has been pointed out) there were no Directors, shareholders, officers or a Common Seal, so there was no authority to dispose of the property. The only answer was a compulsory purchase order.

Notices were fixed on WCPLR property by the council and addressed to the Weston, Clevedon and Portishead Light Railway Company 'and to all other persons having or claiming or enabled to sell any estate or interest in the said lands, demanding from them particulars of their estate and interest therein and the claim made by them in respect thereof and stating that the Council were willing to treat for the purpose thereof'. As was expected, no claims to the fee simple ownership of the lands were received and Compulsory Purchase Orders were made under Section 10(1)(a) of the Town and Country Planning Act of 1944.

On 16th March, 1953 the Weston-super-Mare Borough Council pursuant to the seventy-sixth section of the Land Clauses Consolidation Act 1845, paid the sum of £1400 into the Bank of England in respect of the light railway land appropriated in the borough. The Vesting Deed was signed on 20th March, 1953. The Lands Tribunal determined that £2350 should be compensation for the land and buildings taken over by the Clevedon UDC and this was also paid into the Bank of England. These funds were claimed a few years later, supposedly by British Railways.[9]

In the mid-1950s, two Bristol businessmen, S. Jones Frank and Major W. D. I. Gunn, founded the North Somerset Light Railway Company Limited, with its offices at 57 Queen Square, Bristol, only a few doors from No. 70 where the 1884 company had an office. They hoped to rebuild the light railway on the 2 ft 8 in. gauge between Worle and Clevedon. There was to be a half-mile diversion from the WCPLR roadbed at the Clevedon end in order to reach Salthouse Fields near the sea front. Intermediate halts were planned at Wick St Lawrence and Kingston Seymour. *Septimus*, an 0−4−2 saddle tank engine which had hitherto worked on Pike's Tramway, Purbeck in Dorset, was returned to its makers, Peckett & Company of Bristol, for overhaul and fitting of the vacuum brake, with a view to running on this line, but the project did not reach the practical stage as only a new Act of Parliament could overcome the complicated legal position of the old company and allow the new one to purchase the trackbed. Unfortunately *Septimus* was scrapped by Joseph Pugsley at Peckett's in 1962.

Notes:

1. *The Weston, Clevedon & Portishead Light Railway* by Michael Windeatt, typescript, Clevedon Library, 654828 T 3852
2. PRO RAIL 253/532
3. E. C. Carey
4. E. C. Carey
5. One of the men refused to go
6. *Clevedon Mercury*, 25th May, 1940
7. *Railway Magazine*, 1942 p. 378
8. P. Strange
9. *The Weston, Clevedon & Portishead Railway*, C. Redwood

2–2–2WT locomotive *Weston* seen here with a train for Weston-super-Mare standing at Clevedon Station in the early 1900s. A party of men from St John's Church, Lower Weston, Bath are being photographed as they are about to board from the very low platform.   *J. Weight Collection*

Chapter Eight
Description of the Line

Weston station was situated in Ashcombe Road about three-quarters of a mile from the sea front; in the early days a horse omnibus plying to and fro met all trains. The timber station buildings (not erected until Easter 1898), had an unusual, almost semi-circular corrugated iron roof, the iron fence separating the building from the track, going right up to the sleeper ends and giving very little clearance. The single, short wooden platform only 10 inches above the ground was replaced between 1916 and 1921 by a timber platform of standard height and a small waiting shelter. The company owned No. 88, Ashcombe Road adjacent to the station and painted 'Weston, Clevedon and Portishead Tramway Company' across the downstairs windows, the first floor being used as living accommodation. Not much altered, the house is now a chemist's shop. A cistern supported on posts acted as a water tower.

The original layout had two parallel tracks linked by a crossover at the west end of the platform, but in 1908 the shunting neck was removed from the run-round loop and a siding laid to the east of the station for the use of local coal merchants, milk traffic utilising the special platform provided. Spare coaches were stored here. The playing fields of Lewisham House School were adjacent to the railway. It was said that a football kicked into the bunker of a departing engine could not be retrieved until its return from Portishead, while a cricket ball once passed through an open window into an empty compartment!

The railway passed along the rear of houses to Milton Road halt (1.06 miles). The waiting hut was designed by Col Stephens in 1932 when travelling in the brake van with Guard Carey. Children kicked in the asbestos walls, which were then covered with corrugated iron. The short siding,laid with 40 lb./yd rail, was principally used by coal wagons. Here, as at all level crossings until the 1899 Act allowed the line to be a light railway and protect the track with cattle grids, were level crossing gates. At some locations a keeper worked them in summer, while in winter the gates were opened by the fireman and closed by the guard. Only a quarter of a mile beyond where the line crossed Locking Road, Bristol Road halt (1.32 miles) was opened in 1912, no shelter being provided until 1938 when the halt was re-located on the Weston side of the crossing.

The next station, Worle Town (1.83 miles) seems a curious name today, for the settlement is really only a village. The fact is that Worle was the market town for Weston and a century ago was more important than the watering place. 'Worle' changed to 'Worle (Moor Lane)' in July/August 1913 and to 'Worle Town' November/December 1917, to distinguish it from the Great Western station (which closed 2nd January, 1922). Worle had a booking office, waiting shed rather more grand than those at halts, and a short platform similar to the original one at Weston, but this was later removed. There was a run-round loop with shunting neck and a siding, chiefly used for coal, the siding originally continuing across Station Road to the gas works until its closure in 1921. The coach was left on when shunting,

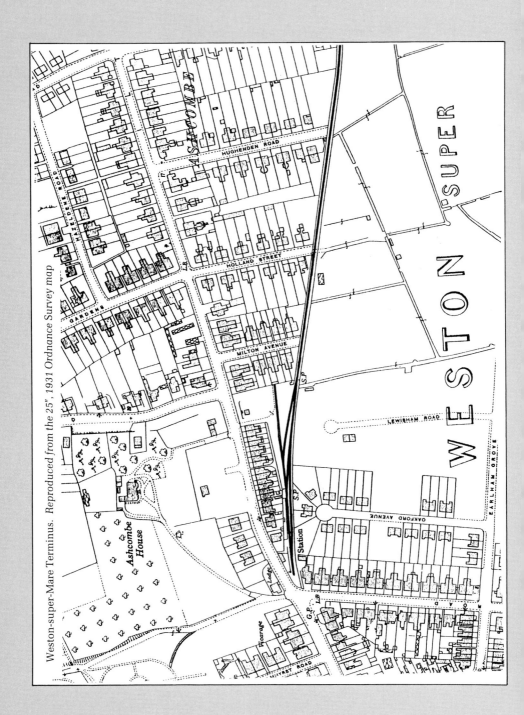

Weston-super-Mare Terminus.   Reproduced from the 25", 1931 Ordnance Survey map

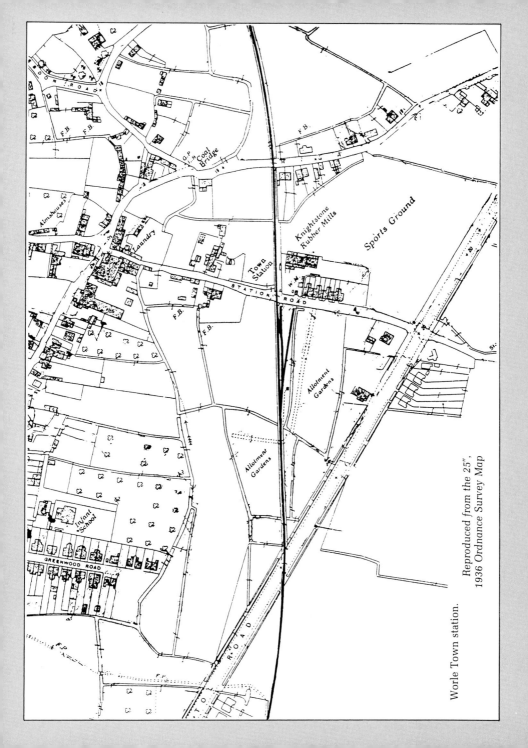

Worle Town station.

Reproduced from the 25",
1936 Ordnance Survey Map

The entrance to Weston-super-Mare station, c.1898. A passenger coach stands on the spur line that was later lifted. A wooden fence marks-out where the street tramway to Milton Road and the Boulevard began. The house (right) was the residence of E.R. Wintour (Traffic Manager) and on its lower windows is printed 'Weston, Clevedon and Portishead Tramways'. The notice board to the left at the entrance to the station building reads, 'Weston & Clevedon Tramway' whilst the curved notice board proclaims 'Lewisham House School Play Ground'.

L.G.R.P., courtesy David and Charles

The 10 inch high platform at Weston-super-Mare seen here in 1908 and which remained until 1919, when new higher platforms were installed. The sleepers are of half-round wooden section and the shunting neck was removed shortly after this photograph was taken. *L.G.R.P., courtesy David and Charles*

The unusual style of the Weston-super-Mare station office building. Notice the luggage cart (*right*), the large gas lamps, and the water tower (*left*).

E.H. Hazell, courtesy J.J. Herd

Locomotive *Portishead* arriving at Weston-super-Mare on 10th August, 1935. Note the coal wagons standing in the siding near the rear of the train. *R.W. Kidner*

The large Drewry railcar No. 5 alongside the wooden waiting shelter at Weston-super-Mare station, *c.*1937.   *M.E.J. Deane*

A further view of Weston-super-Mare station *c.*1935; note the wagons in sidings and the small Drewry petrol-driven railcar.   *M.E.J. Deane*

Milton Road halt with coal wagons in the 130 yards-long siding. This view was taken looking towards Weston-super-Mare in February 1938 and shows the diminutive waiting shelter constructed of asbestos. This halt was situated just over 1 mile from Weston. *L.G.R.P., courtesy David and Charles*

The level crossing traffic lights installed on the Locking Road seen here in March 1938. This crossing was called Locking Road whereas the halt was called 'Bristol Road'. *L.G.R.P., courtesy David and Charles*

The all-wood station at Worle, seen pre-1913, before 'Town' was added to the name board in 1917. The station master has a WC&PR badge on his cap. Note the P.O. wagon in the siding to the gas works, whilst the Worle Coal Company's office can be seen above the fence. This view shows the low wooden platform which had been removed by the 1920s.   *W. Hembury Collection*

Locomotive *Portishead* seen *c.*1932 with a train from Weston-super-Mare comprising the Metropolitan coach and LSWR set at Worle Town.   *K.E. Hackett*

The small Wick St Lawrence station and single lever ground frame, *c.*1920.
Miss F. Chaplin Collection

An earlier view in 1910 of Wick St Lawrence showing the larger door opening. This view towards Clevedon shows the signals on short posts. This station was treated as the halfway passing loop between Clevedon and Weston. *Dickens/Maggs Collection*

Locomotive No. 4 seen on an August Bank Holiday special to Weston-super-Mare approaching Wick St Lawrence bridge in August 1938.   *P. Strange*

Railcar No. 5 and trailer on the Weston-super-Mare to Clevedon train, crossing the bridge over the River Yeo in June 1937.   *L.G.R.P., courtesy David and Charles*

An early view, *c.*1899, of Kingston Road Crossing with the permanent way gang installing the cattle grid. A milk platform was established here for local farmers but removed in the 1930s.   *G. Rushton Collection*

Broadstone halt seen here in June 1937. This halt did not appear in the timetables before 1918 and had room for a siding to be constructed, but this was never built. The timetable seen in the shelter hut is dated 16th September, 1936. Notice the use of sleepers and angled wood forming the cattle grid.

L.G.R.P., courtesy David and Charles

A mixed train to Clevedon, leaving Kingston Road halt 1935, including a Rose, Smith & Co. coal wagon. *R.W. Kidner*

Colehouse Lane, June 1937. The original shelter, shown here, is of a long narrow construction to fit between the track and the hedge (the cattle grid was positioned to the left). John Capell features in this photograph, whose father was a solicitor at Weston and sold the station site there to the railway.

L.G.R.P., courtesy David and Charles

The new shelter at Colehouse Lane, now situated on the north side of the line, viewed towards Clevedon in March 1939.
P. Strange

the operation sometimes taking nearly half-an-hour and making children late for school. Miss Florence Radford was station mistress and dealt with a considerable number of parcels.

Ebdon Lane (3.09 miles) had a milk platform until the early thirties, Wick St Lawrence (3.8 miles) also having a milk platform and shelter. Wick was a passing place at which single line staffs were exchanged, train crews working points and signals. Staff and ticket boxes were provided, pink tickets for the section to Weston and green to Clevedon, being kept in boxes screwed to the desk in the office section of the station building. Trains ceased to cross here in 1915 and the primitive signals with slotted posts and solid finials were also removed. The siding at Wick was later used for wagon storage. The village of Wick St Lawrence nearly a mile from the station was completely dependent on the WCPLR for transport to the outside world, both for passengers and goods traffic. The manager of a Weston-super-Mare bank lived at Wick and if he was not at the station in the morning, a member of the train crew called at his home for him, passengers being kept waiting while he shaved, this again making children late for school. On Friday mornings Wick people took chickens to butchers with no extra fare being charged. Bundles of newspapers from Barnes's shop opposite the station at Weston-super-Mare, were thrown out by the guard at Wick if the train did not stop, villagers collecting their own paper from the shed.

Beyond the station a spur led to the Yeo Wharf used by traffic from South Wales which was mainly carried in sailing barges. The main line rose on a gradient of 1 in 230 to the bridge over the River Yeo which was a seven span structure of 240 ft in length, 30 ft above the river bed and giving a headway

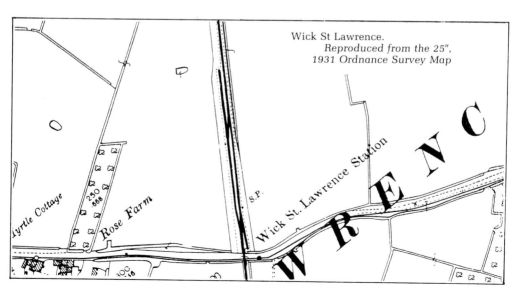

Wick St Lawrence.
*Reproduced from the 25",
1931 Ordnance Survey Map*

Clevedon station looking towards Portishead, in 1921 with the GWR brick-built stables (*right*) behind the WCPLR building. The station buildings consisted of a waiting room, booking office and toilets. Note the fitter's cottage alongside the crossing.   *E.H. Hazell, courtesy H. Carey*

The station office at Clevedon. The water softener can be seen (*centre*) and the timber-clad water tank beyond; the platform is in the distance on the right.   *E.H. Hazell*

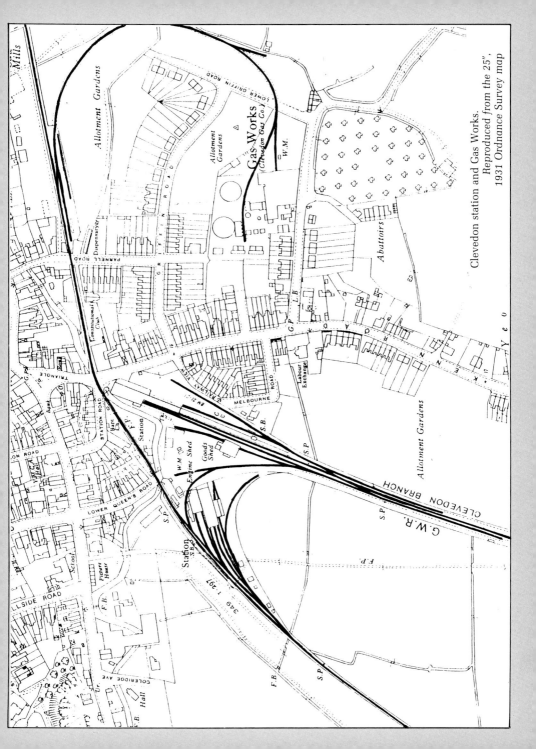

Clevedon station and Gas Works.
Reproduced from the 25"
1931 Ordnance Survey map

of 2 ft above HWOST. Built of lattice girders on cast iron piers it was painted with tar. The two piers nearest Clevedon sank soon after erection, the dip needing timber supports. In 1907 Handyside & Company of Derby undertook certain repairs, while in the thirties, the WCPLR pile driver was used to strengthen it. A train crossing the bridge made the bridge judder and some passengers felt nervous, particularly when the tide was in, though the structure was reportedly quite stable. Check rails inside both running rails guarded against derailing. Beyond the bridge (which was level) the gradient fell at 1 in 200.

Mud Lane Crossing had a sleeper-built milk platform as did Ham Lane halt (4.93 miles), the latter having a siding at which locally cut peat was loaded. Broadstone halt (5.25 miles) opened in 1918 had a small wooden hut like those used by roadmen, to shelter waiting passengers. Both these halts were only a mile from the village of Kingston Seymour. The country round about is very low-lying and a wall keeps the sea from flooding the land. Kingston Road halt (5.95 miles) also had a milk platform and just beyond the line crossed the River Kenn. Colehouse Lane halt (6.8 miles) had a long and narrow shelter moved nearer Clevedon in March 1939 when its original site was required by the BBC to make an entrance to its transmitting station. About midway between here and Clevedon, trailing points to the east led to a siding,[1] perhaps used for peat working or the brick works on the Strode Road, but not *in situ* for long. The line crossed the River Middle Yeo and approached Clevedon station (7.85 miles), headquarters of the railway.

The loop at this important intermediate station had only a single timber platform, originally only 10 inches high, but by 1921 raised to standard level. Although a passing place from 1907 (when the Portishead extension was opened) Clevedon retained its original single platform, necessitating the inconvenience of one train having to complete station work, draw out and reverse into the loop in order to permit the other to come in. In addition to the waiting shelter on the platform, the station also had the refinements of a ladies' room and booking office off the end of the platform, and as at Weston, the unusual semi-circular roof and iron fence between the building and track. A water tower was placed at each end of the platform.

Opposite the station were the locomotive and carriage sheds. The former measured 60 ft by 20 ft and 14 ft high, one road holding two engines and the other, three. The original carriage shed was 80 ft by 15 ft and 14 ft high but received an addition on its south side, making a total of three roads. All sheds had wooden sides and ends, were roofed with galvanised iron and glass and housed locomotives, but not coaches, and shielded by sliding doors. A sand-drying store and carpenters' shop were at the back of the sheds which were adjacent and shared a common wall. Power for the 8 in. centre lathe, shaper and drilling machine in the repair shops was supplied by a Crossley Otto 8 hp gas engine operating from the town gas supply. A water softening plant was added in 1921 when the old tanks over the engine shed road were removed.

An end-on connection via a sharp curve was made with a mileage siding in the Great Western yard. It did not appear in the Railway Clearing House Junction Diagrams of 1914 and was probably not used after 1924, the points

A good general view of Clevedon station taken on the 21st August, 1937. The line
to the right runs into the engine shed.   *A.W. Croughton*

Locomotive No. 5 at Clevedon.

Author's Collection

A fine view of *Weston* at Clevedon in 1907 outside the locomotive shed. A Napier & Co. P.O. wagon on the Great Western siding can be seen at the far right. (Notice the original water tanks to the left of the locomotive.) *W. Hembury Collection*

The Clevedon coaling stage seen in 1927 with locomotive *Weston* (*left*), the second tractor A137 and *Hesperus* beyond. This view gives a good impression of the water softening plant. *Photomatic Ltd*

Clevedon sheds in August 1940 after the closure of the WCPLR. The only locomotive is 'Terrier' No. 4, on the left, and two open wagons share the accommodation.

H.C. Casserley

A fine view of the running track (on concrete blocks) at Clevedon. Note the store (*left*) for both concrete and timber sleepers, fitter Hill lived in the house on the right. The level crossing cabin can be seen in distance, left of the track, just before the gate.

E.H. Hazell

The turnout to the gas works siding (*right*), Clevedon, December 1936, viewed towards Clevedon East. Note Parnell Road Goods siding on the right.   *P. Strange*

Locomotive No. 4 propelling wagons into Clevedon Gas Works in 1937. The stock (*left to right*) comprises a Tar wagon; three Clevedon Gas Company wagons; S.C. (Stephenson Clarke) wagon; Clevedon Gas Company wagon and S.C. wagon.

P. Strange

No. 1 *Clevedon* leaving Clevedon gas works with a load of empties in September 1937 with guard Dan Carey riding in the cab steps.   *P. Strange*

Clevedon Gas Company wagon No. 21. Although the picture is dated June 1932, this P.O. wagon was not new, as it was constructed during the World War I period and therefore refurbished for the Gas Co.   *H. Carey Collection*

in this rarely used connection being recovered by the GWR in 1936. Its 130 ft radius curve was probably the reason for WCPLR six-coupled engines at one period running with one pair of wheels uncoupled. There was a considerable risk of derailment due to wagon buffers interlocking, but the American-type bogie coaches must have been delivered via this curve as the extension to Portishead and the junction there with the GWR had yet to be built. It is possible that their tramway design may have let them negotiate tight curves. Wagons exchanged at Clevedon were eased round the curve with a pinch bar, this method reducing the risk of derailment. Exchange traffic at Clevedon was mostly inwards for the Light Railway's own use, the GWR imposing a charge of three shillings per vehicle. To give access to the WCPLR all but three or four of the 17 wagons occupying the siding were required to be drawn out.

The GWR said[2] that although the junction was not really fit for traffic purposes, it did not mind it being used for transfer if the WCPLR was willing to tolerate the risk, locomotives transferred being derailed and coaches damaged. Any vehicle being exchanged was required to be placed in a rake as a Great Western engine could not negotiate the sharp curve. In 1907 the GWR reported exchange traffic light, except in the early years of the century when Worle Gas Company were carrying out extensions and alterations. GWR gas tanks were placed just on the Great Western side of the gate to charge WCPLR coaches and in 1907 the GWR was somewhat peeved when a gas tank wagon was taken from Bristol to Clevedon, and then not used, as the gas coaches were only used for daylight working. In 1922 a siding was laid by the WCPLR which was to form a connection with the GWR's shunting spur and would thus have offered an easier curve for exchange. Never completed, the Light Railway section of the siding was used for wagon storage.

Beyond the Lower Queen's Road level crossing was a much more complicated crossing in front of the GWR station, the three large gates being lever-worked by a gatekeeper from his picturesque cabin. It was impossible to site it in such a position that he could have a clear view of each street, and as the largest gate closed over the road unseen from his cabin, a warning bell sounded before the gate moved, but this precaution did not prevent unattended cars from being struck by it. The gates failed to block the railway completely, so after closing them, the crossing keeper walked in front of the train holding two flags: a red flag with which to restrain impatient cyclists and pedestrians, and a green flag to wave the train on at the statutory 4 mph. Between trains the gateboy cleaned coaches. As the train crossed the road, it also crossed the curiously named River Land Yeo and squeezed between it and the Clevedon Engineering Company on the north side and the Constitutional Club on the other.

Parnell Road goods yard was beyond with its few coal pens and three North Eastern Railway box van bodies for dry storage. A private siding a quarter of a mile in length led to Clevedon Gasworks (incorporated in 1856), an attractive rural section being encountered *en route*. Because it was a facing siding, an engine pushed wagons from Clevedon to the works. The

A poor but important view of All Saints' level crossing, *c.*1908.

H. Carey Collection

The rustic Walton Park halt, *c.*1935, view towards Portishead. Note the passenger waiting on the 'rails' for the next service! *W.H. Harbor Collection*

Walton in Gordano, view towards Portishead, October 1938. This halt was situated in the heart of the picturesque Gordano Valley, now a conservation area.

Author's Collection

The 10.15 am Portishead to Weston-super-Mare headed by No. 5, arriving at Cadbury Road on 15th February, 1936. A siding was situated to the south and used in World War I for unloading manure from Avonmouth Remount Depot for local farmers.

Author's Collection

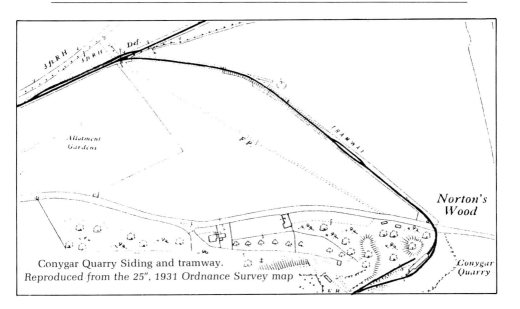

Conygar Quarry Siding and tramway.
Reproduced from the 25", 1931 Ordnance Survey map

company's two wagons, Nos. 100 and 101 painted red with white lettering shaded black were both destroyed on 13th October, 1928 in the Charfield disaster on the LMS between Bristol and Gloucester. They were replaced by 12 wagons (probably numbered 21 to 32) grey with white lettering and on their arrival at Clevedon the manager was so proud of them that they were given two coats of varnish.[3] They were also used, together with the WCPLR's own wagons, for bringing coal from Wick St Lawrence Wharf. The gasworks also owned a rectangular tank wagon No. 1 which conveyed tar to Butler's Chemical Works, Bristol, occasionally Butler's own tanks being used. Periodically Clevedon Gas Company's No. 1 was filled with ammonical liquour which was sprayed over the WCPLR track formation as a weed killer. *Circa* 1938 the GWR weedkilling train of 2500 gallon tenders, travelled over the Light Railway hauled by 'Terrier' No. 4[4]. Shell Mex and Berry Wiggins also sent tar tanks to the gas works. From time to time the works received a consignment of cast iron pipes from Stanton Ironworks. The siding belonged to the company and was still *in situ* in 1961, as was the weighbridge.

Beyond Parnell Road yard was a facing siding on the left, originally laid in 1917 to serve the Munition Box Works[5] and when hostilities ceased, this became Shopland's saw mills. Shopland's obtained most of their timber locally, hauling it with their own traction engines. The siding was lifted *circa* 1923.

Clevedon East (8.54 miles) by a gated level crossing, had a waiting shelter and a siding to Weech's Joinery Works (owned by the joinery works). Wagons of timber came from Cardiff. This siding was still *in situ* in 1956. As consignments of 20 or more wagons arrived for Weech's and their sidings only held seven, some were left in the loop at Walton Park, and others at Clevedon and in the Walton-in-Gordano loop.[6] The line at East Clevedon was very near Clevedon Court, one of the most perfect examples of medieval domestic architecture in Britain and the home of Sir Edmund Elton, Chairman of the CUDC and a WCPLR shareholder. The house was the 'Castlewood' in Thackeray's novel, *Esmond*.

Beyond East Clevedon the railway climbed on a gradient of 1 in 116 twisting through the picturesque and well-named Swiss Valley. All Saints' halt (8.77 miles) was opened 1917.[7] The crossing had two sets of gates — a pair for All Saints' Lane and another pair for Walton Road. Like those at the Triangle they were operated by levers rather than a wheel and difficulty was sometimes experienced opening the gates in a strong wind. They were worked by blacksmith Sam Harris and his son Sam Harris junior, (whose shop was opposite the crossing) the pay being £1 1s. 0d. a week — excellent remuneration for a part time job in those days.

Beyond the crossing was a 300 yd climb at 1 in 68 and it was not unknown for long trains, such as Sunday School specials, to be divided to enable them to ascend the incline.

Just beyond the line's summit, Walton Park halt (9.23 miles) with a shelter like a garden summer house, was situated on a gradient of 1 in 50 'down', towards Portishead. The siding was made into a loop in 1919. During the nineteen-thirties bogie bolsters laden with pipes from Stanton Iron Works arrived for unloading, as did telegraph poles on the same type of wagon.[8] Another siding, capable of holding 35 wagons, led to Conygar Quarry, passengers having to wait patiently while the engine shunted this siding. A narrow gauge tramway linked the quarry with the concrete platform where the tram wagons were tipped into BQC standard gauge wagons painted red with white lettering shaded black, a few being early steel ones, standing below. A length of track at the far end of the siding still lies in position looking remarkably good after being out of use for fifty years. The narrow gauge tippers were pushed by hand across Clapton Road from the crusher plant to the top of an inclined plane and sent down in groups of three controlled by a winding drum near the road. Empties were hauled up by an electric winch. The quarry produced dressed pennant stone for kerbs, steps and seats with block stone for rebuilding Temple Meads station in the nineteen-thirties coming from this quarry. Although it has been stated that the quarry owned two standard gauge locomotives,[9] it is believed that this was not, in fact, the case. Conygar Quarries were owned and worked until 1924 by Sandford & Conygar Quarries Company, a subsidiary of the Teign Valley Granite Company Limited which in due course was parent to Roads Reconstruction Limited.[10]

Through the Gordano Valley the line ran on a low embankment, still extant, parallel with the B3124 road, falling at 1 in 94 to Walton-in-Gordano (9.92 miles), this, too, having a looped siding (opened in 1926) with concrete slabs forming a loading bay. Cadbury Road halt (11.42 miles) probably

Black Rock Quarries transfer siding, 1921. The nearest standard gauge wagon is owned by the Lancashire & Yorkshire Railway, with GWR and MR wagons standing behind. On the loading bank is one of the quarry company's 2 ft gauge Hudswell, Clarke 0−6−0WTs.   *E.H. Hazell*

The Clevedon to Portishead train approaching Black Rock Quarry sidings on 22nd September, 1937.   *P. Strange, courtesy C. Redwood*

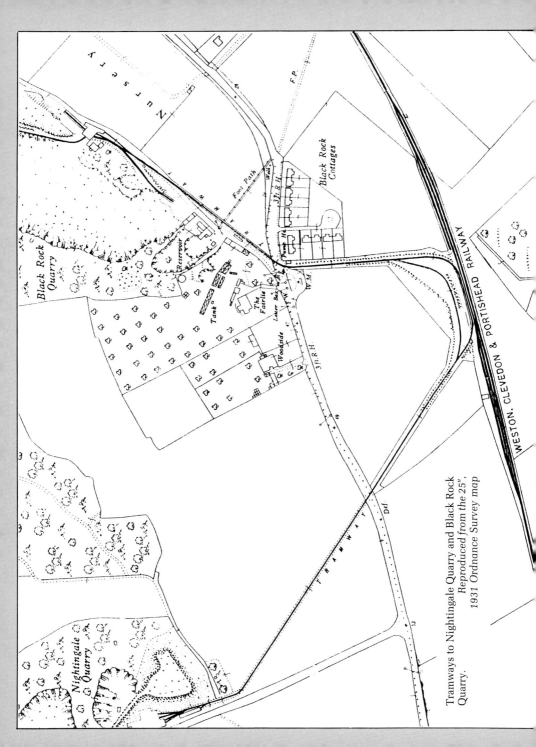

Tramways to Nightingale Quarry and Black Rock Quarry.
Reproduced from the 25", 1931 Ordnance Survey map

received this name to encourage tourists who would then enjoy the hike of 1½ miles and climb of 300 ft to Cadbury Camp, a stronghold of the Ancient Britons. Cadbury Road really served the village of Weston-in-Gordano and soon after the opening of the extension to Portishead one traveller wrote a strongly worded letter to the *Clevedon Mercury*. He objected to Weston-in-Gordano halt being called Cadbury Road, saying that in the village he was told that the station was really in Moor Lane. Although authorised by the Light Railway Commissioners on 12th August, 1911, the siding was probably not put in until World War I when it was used for distributing horse manure from the remount depot at Shirehampton on the Clifton Down to Avonmouth line. Although only 5¼ miles away as the crow flies, it was four times the distance by rail.

Less than half a mile beyond Cadbury Road halt were Black Rock Quarry sidings holding 90 wagons, consisting of a siding opened in 1919, made into a loop later that year to facilitate traffic working, further sidings being laid in 1931. The sidings were served by narrow gauge lines from two quarries: Nightingale to the west and Black Rock itself to the east. Half way along the loop in a shallow cutting was a loading platform. This was a concrete shelf built out from a retaining wall of the same material so as partly to overhang the track. Tram wagons on the shelf could be tipped sideways discharging straight into standard gauge wagons standing below.

Black Rock Quarries registered as a limited company c.1918; Bryant & Langford Quarries Limited being formed in 1925 to merge it with other quarrying interests of this Bristol-based company. In due course it became one of the constituents of Roads Reconstruction (1934) Limited. Roads Reconstruction were still operating 132 twelve ton wagons all in the livery of black, with white lettering shaded red, in 1946. They were probably steel-lined wagons used for tarred roadstone and thus exempt from wartime pooling arrangements.[11] Bute Works wagons were also used. Clean crushed stone travelled in common user wagons, or GWR ballast hoppers if the contract was for that company. Most of the Clevedon to Portishead trains were steam hauled so that they could stop at the quarry and attach up to about 10 loaded trucks at the rear, a total of 40 wagons or more being dealt with during a busy day. 1934 saw an average of 75 wagons daily from Black Rock and Conygar quarries, this traffic bringing in an income of £3050 compared with £750 from passenger receipts and £422 from other services. At Portishead the wagons were placed on the weighbridge and then propelled to the GWR exchange siding. Stone from Conygar tended to be destined for Toton, and that from Black Rock to Acton and Hayes.[12] Similarly Portishead to Clevedon trains took empty wagons to the quarry sidings in addition to tar and bitumen tankers and coal for liquifying these substances, Key's oil tank wagon No. 10 regularly running from their works at Portishead Docks to the quarry with residual oil for making asphalt.[13]

The 2 ft gauge quarry system operated until about 1949. Its first two locomotives were Hudswell, Clarke 0−6−0 well tanks, Works Nos. 1377/8, originally 60cm gauge engines built for the War Department as Nos. 3207/8, and were sent to the Leighton Buzzard Light Railway on 31st May, 1919. The centre pair of wheels was flangeless. Arriving from Leighton Buzzard

Portishead South, looking towards Portishead in June 1937, showing the standard style waiting shelter.

L.G.R.P., courtesy David and Charles

Portishead station taken on the opening day, 7th August, 1907 with No. 3 *Weston* running round its train. On the left, the temporary connection with the GWR has been discontinued. The stop block was later removed and level crossing gates replaced the frail-looking fence. Later Mustad's nail factory was built in the field on the left.

M.J. Tozer Collection

*c.*1922, No. 3207 was sold to R. Fielding & Son, Blackpool in 1925. Subsequent power was provided by four-wheeled internal combustion engined machines, the Motor Rail Simplex locomotives arriving with armour plating.[14]

Builder	Works No.	Date	Previous History	Disposal
Motor Rail Ltd	400	1917	Was WD light railway No. 2121	To Roads Reconstruction Cranmore Depot and scrapped *c.*1955
Motor Rail Ltd	587	1917	Was WD light railway No. 2308. Black Rock purchased it from S. Pearson & Sons Ltd, contractors	As above
Motor Rail Ltd	1699	1918	Was WD light railway No. 2420	Sold or scrapped
Kerr, Stuart	4427	1929	Purchased new	To Roads Reconstruction Cranmore Depot and scrapped *c.*1957
Crossley		?		As above

The next halt was placed at another level crossing, Clapton Road (12.8 miles), Portishead South with its timber shed was situated at 13.09 miles, the trailing siding here being lengthened from 150 to 250 ft between 1915 and 1931. Coal arrived and brick and tiles were shipped out from the adjacent works. The railway crossed two rhines and arrived at Portishead (13.76 miles) with a 4 in. high metalled platform 200 ft in length. Buildings comprised a timber waiting shed, booking office and ladies' room, in very

WESTON CLEVEDON & PORTISHEAD RAILWAY.

N.º 287 Train Staff Ticket between Wick St. Lawrence & Clevedon.

Train No .. ..

To the Engine Driver.

You are authorised **after seeing** *the Train* **Staff** *for the Section to proceed from* **Wick St Lawrence to Clevedon** *and the Train Staff will* **follow.**

Signature of person in charge.................................

....*Station.*

.... 193 ..

(See instructions at back hereof).

Portishead station.
*Reproduced from the 25",
1931 Ordnance Survey map*

rustic architecture, looking very much like a garden summer house, with low trellis decorating the roof, and it qualified as being the line's most attractive station. It was low-lying, a flood on 16th December, 1910 covering the track and making the approach impassable. There was a run-round loop, mileage siding and a private siding to Messrs Mustad's nail works which received consignments of coiled iron in one to three box vans, the finished article also being dispatched by rail. The junction with the GWR was 22 chains beyond the WCPLR station. Most of the traffic exchanged arriving on the light railway was coal, mainly from the East Midlands collieries of Bilsthorpe, Blackwell and Shireoaks, with smaller tonnages from Trentham, Staffordshire. Much of the coal was for Clevedon gas works, with a smaller proportion for merchants at Clevedon, Worle, Milton Road and Weston-super-Mare. Coal traffic was carried in private owners' wagons. Periodically fertiliser arrived consigned to various destinations. Despite being primitive in many respects, one of the WCPLR's modernities was an electric pump which automatically filled the water tank at Portishead.

Notes:

1. OS 1/2500 Sheet 4/11 1902 edition
2. PRO: RAIL 253/528 GWR document H. Griffiths to C. Kislingbury 2nd Sept., 1907
3. Recollection of E. C. Carey
4. Recollection of Howard Carey
5. PRO MT6 2453/14
6. Howard Carey
7. First mentioned in *Bradshaw* October 1917
8. Howard Carey
9. *Industrial Locomotives of South Western England.* Industrial Railway Society.
10. Letter from Dick Kelham to author
11. *Ibid.*
12. E. C. Carey
13. *Ibid.*
14. *Industrial Locomotives of South Western England.* Industrial Railway Society.

Locomotive No. 4 with the last train consisting of Cars Nos. 2 & 4 arriving at Weston-super-Mare on the 18th May, 1940. Note the passengers carrying gasmasks, and the gas lights situated on the station.   *W. Hembury Collection*

Portishead station portrayed on the 21st August, 1937. Notice that only the top of the fence is white. Presumably it has been painted for safety reasons to make it stand out to prevent passengers walking into it.   *A.W. Croughton*

The small railcar arriving at Portishead; notice the petrol tank fixed to the outside of the railcar. There is a ground frame to the right and Messrs Mustad's nail factory and siding to the left.   *R. Lyle*

Portishead station buildings in April 1921. Note the interesting pattern made by rustic work. The accommodation consisted of a waiting room, booking office and ladies' waiting room.   *E.H. Hazell, courtesy J.J. Herd*

A 1920s view of the entrance to Portishead station with the ex-Metropolitan coach on the left. Mustad's nail factory can be seen beyond.   *Author's Collection*

Portishead *c.*1912 with Frank Beere (station master) centre. Note the beautifully ornate chocolate machine.   *H. Carey Collection*

Locomotive No. 5 on the exchange line from the GWR at Portishead in 1935 with guard Jack Riddick on the steps.   *M.E.J. Deane*

Locomotive *Portishead* at Portishead, 1927. Note the small water tower, *right*, with level crossing gate on far right giving access to the GWR system.   *Photomatic Ltd*

Chapter Nine

The Wick St Lawrence Wharf Branch

The wharf line was built c. 1913[1] for the purpose of developing sea traffic to and from South Wales. Land for building the branch was sold to Heath acting as Trustee for the Excess Insurance Company, costs being:[2]

	£	s.	d.
Purchase of land	586	13	0
Erection of landing stage, crane etc.	1880	15	3
Restoration	705	14	9
Paid to railway for materials etc.	350	0	0
Berth for vessels	35	0	0

The portion of foreshore occupied by the jetty was owned by the Trustees of the Queen Elizabeth's Hospital Foundation, Bristol, who leased it to the Excess Insurance Company for an annual rent of a pound.[3] No Parliamentary sanction was required for building the line. The wharf itself was a concrete platform only 4 in. thick and 12 ft wide supported on concrete and timber piles, carrying a line of rail, raised on a concrete ramp. When driving the piles, it was necessary to go twice as deep into the clay as expected. The railway shipped much of its coal supplies from Newport, Barry, or Penarth, (coal coming from Tirpentwys Colliery, Pontypool, in the nineteen-thirties), to the wharf, where it was transferred into WCPLR trucks by steam crane. In 1931 the crane became life expired and stored on a nearby siding, from then on coal being shovelled by hand into baskets or big steel buckets and raised by ship's derrick.

Weight restrictions only permitted three wagons on the wharf at a time and they were either dragged off by steel hawser attached to the tractor, or eased off by pinch bar. The wagons were then picked up by service train and for convenience were usually pushed to Clevedon, the guard riding on the front wagon. A train could then consist of: coal wagons; locomotive; coaches and tail traffic. All coal loaded into wagons at Wick was taken to Portishead for weighing on the WCPLR's weighbridge there and then brought back to Clevedon, because the Light Railway would not pay the Clevedon Gas Company sixpence a wagon to weigh it on their bridge.[4] For the benefit of the steam crane and to guard against a locomotive at the wharf running short of water, a tank was provided filled by a wind pump.

Although Clevedon Gas Works received some tonnage by this route, most came from the Midlands (via Portishead) and the wharf only had a vessel every few months. Several motor barge captains refused to unload until they were paid and if the cash was not forthcoming, returned to South Wales with the coal.

The Light Railway tried to develop traffic to the wharf and displayed notices 'Seaborne traffic can now be dealt with at Wick St Lawrence' on its timetables and buildings, but it was far from being a commercial success.

The last sailing barge owned by the company was the *Lily*,[5] a 33-tonner with auxiliary motor registered at Barnstaple in the name of Colonel Stephens. Her end was dramatic. On 8th June, 1929 she left Newport for the 20-mile trip across the Bristol Channel to Wick. In her hold was about 30

A general view of the Wick St Lawrence wharf in 1921, showing the mobile crane and piledriver. The bridge, left, carries the main WCPLR Weston to Clevedon line. The jetty was 190 ft in length with a further landing stage of 80 ft. Note the water tower, for filling the steam crane and the storage sheds.   *E.H. Hazell*

The jetty crane in the siding at Wick St Lawrence, May 1937.   *P. Strange*

tons of coal. Almost as soon as she had left the shelter of the River Usk, her crew of two spotted a trickle of dirty black water on the floor of the forward cable locker. They lashed the helm and both took to the pumps. To return to Newport would have been the best plan, but this was quite out of the question because of the direction of the tide. Tom Betteridge and Jack Hunter continued their struggle at the pumps, but the Somerset shore seemed to get no closer as the hours went by. Eventually *Lily* had so much water inside her that she failed to answer the helm. Fortunately the sea was practically calm.

Lily drifted past Flat Holm, narrowly missing its rocky shore and continued on into Barry Roads. The tide began to turn and the crew saw with relief that they were drifting back towards the Usk. They let out the anchor and continued pumping. The effort proved too much for Captain Betteridge and he collapsed. While Jack Hunter was busy reviving him, the Newport cutter *Fancy* saw their desperate plight and offered to tow. This they gladly accepted and a warp was passed between them.

The strain was too great for poor old *Lily*. Her weakened timbers slowly opened. Suddenly she settled much deeper. There was only one thing left to do. Quickly Jack dived overboard, followed by the captain. Half a minute later, *Lily* rose stem first, turned right over on her bow quarter and sank to the bottom with coal falling out of her hold.

Another vessel seen at Wick was the ketch *Edith*, registered at Bridgwater by Howell Bryant and Captain Sidney Warren. Sold in 1927 she was re-registered at Bridgwater by Renwick, Wilton & Company, the Torquay coal merchants. Small steam coasters also put in an appearance and some stone traffic was exported.

Notes:

1. Recollection of Arthur Westcott
2. *Clevedon Mercury*, 9th August, 1924
3. C. Redwood
4. E. C. Carey
5. *Somerset Harbours*. G. Farr

A one coach train hauled by *Hesperus* (as yet unnamed) seen at Weston-super-Mare in 1911. Note George Newton in his straw boater.   *M.J. Tozer Collection*

A good view of locomotive *Clevedon* with its train to Weston-super-Mare, consisting of two close-coupled ex-LSWR coaches, seen here approaching Wick St Lawrence in June 1937.   *L.G.R.P., courtesy David and Charles*

Locomotive No. 2 *Portishead* at Portishead with the Metropolitan coach set, *c.*1935. Note the tall LBSCR lamp brackets at the front, and the bottle jack on the footplate near the coal bunker.   *Lens of Sutton*

Chapter Ten
Permanent Way and Signalling

Standard gauge was adopted so that there could be through running to and from the GWR without transhipment and as the line did not abound in sharp curves, there was little to be gained by adopting narrow gauge. Only a single line with passing loops was laid. The line from Weston to Clevedon was laid with 56 lb./yd flat bottomed rails 30 ft in length spiked to transverse half round sleepers, soon replaced by those of conventional rectangular section. When Stephens took over the line he found that while under the original Act 56 lb./yd rails were authorised, under the Schedule attached to a later Light Railway Order, a minimum of 58 lb was required. Wishing to regularise the position, he contacted the Board of Trade, the Light Railway Commissioners agreeing that 56 lb. rail would suffice for a 12 ton axle load subject to a maximum speed of 25 mph. The width at formation level was 13 ft and the space between the lines, sidings and passing loops 6 ft. The ballast for the Clevedon to Portishead section was broken stone from Black Rock Quarry of a rather finer grade than the 'Big Four' used and 9 in. deep, while that used between Clevedon and Weston was pennant stone from Conygar Quarry.

In 1919 the company started manufacturing concrete blocks at Clevedon to replace defective wooden sleepers with a more durable material. Measuring 12 in. by 20 in. by 6 in., they were set at 2 ft 2 in. spacing when supporting 65 lb./yd flat bottomed rail, but when utilised for 80 lb./yd rail, two additional blocks were used for each 30 ft length. The maximum axle load for 65 lb./yd rail was 14 tons and 18 tons for 80 lb.yd. A wooden trenail was placed in the hole in the concrete block to receive the rail fasteners, either dogs driven into the trenails, or fangbolts fitted in holes bored in the plugs. Ties, generally made from old point rodding, were fitted four to a 30 ft rail, or as often as found desirable, dependent on curvature and other factors. The concrete blocks were cast in ordinary moulds and did not require any special process. Men produced them when other work was impracticable due to rain or other causes, one ton of cement making about 86 blocks. One of the earliest applications of concrete blocks to replace defective sleepers was the stretch of track at Clevedon between Lower Queen's Road and the Triangle, which was laid solely with these blocks, every other pair (and adjacent pairs at rail joints), joined by tie rods. After World War II when Meadow Road housing estate was built on the site of Parnell Road goods yard, 50 tons of these concrete blocks needed to be moved by a contractor.

From 1922 until 1938, 2525 cubic yards of ballast, 12½ miles of fencing, 13,183 sleepers and 13 tons of rail were replaced. There were two permanent way gangs, one based at Clevedon and the other at Weston-super-Mare.

Fence posts 4 ft 6 in. in height on the Portishead section, supported six wires with three intermediate droppers every 24 ft. There were 80 level crossings between Weston and Portishead ranging from farm occupation to road crossings. Most of the latter were ungated with cattle grids. These were strips of wood, 12 ft by 6 in. by 4½ in. by 4½ in., painted white, placed 2 in. apart parallel to the rails. In the days of the steam tramway when the gates were in use, women gatekeepers were employed to open and close them, but in winter, the cheaper expedient was adopted of the fireman opening the gates and the conductor shutting them.

After the early days when there was only one engine in steam and indeed only one engine, a train staff was used in connection with Annett's Patent Locking Apparatus. Up and down trains met at the Wick St Lawrence loop and exchanged staffs. A novel feature here was that there were no signal lamps, a strong headlight on the engine enabling the driver to see the signals. During winter when the line reverted to 'one engine in steam', the loop was out of use and the line worked as single throughout. The train staff and ticket was combined with a 'telephone block'. There were starting and home signals at each terminus and stop signals at the entrances to the Wick loop. Clevedon, Wick, Worle and Weston were the only places with signals until 1907, points interlocking with them either directly, or by means of keys controlled by the frames. Ticket boxes were in use at Portishead, Clevedon, Wick St Lawrence and Weston-super-Mare so that in each section trains could be dispatched in the same direction under staff and ticket regulations, provided the staff was held by the forwarding station.

A letter sent by the WCPLR to the Board of Trade on 19th May, 1908 explained the signalling arrangements at Clevedon. This being the head-quarters, it was where trains were made up, and all started or finished here. A run-round road gave access to the engine shed and carriage siding. This road and the main running road were controlled by a pointsman in a hut at the west end of the passenger platform who received the section staff as each train arrived and issued the appropriate staff (Portishead or Wick St Lawrence) to the driver of each departing train. On 5th January, 1909 Colonel von Donop on behalf of the Board of Trade inspected and passed the home signal at each end of Clevedon station. The signal and siding points were worked from a ground frame of two levers at either end of the station. At the end of 1920[1] the Westinghouse Brake & Signal Company installed its 4-lever 1914 'E' type frame under the water tower at the Portishead end of the station. It worked up and down home signals and points while there was also a 'home made' signal by the water tank at the Weston end of the station, not interlocked with points. Soon after closure of the Bideford, Westward Ho! & Appledore Railway on 28th March, 1917, Stephens acquired its signalling system and installed their standard McKenzie & Holland signals at Weston, Clevedon and Portishead. Turnouts were controlled by nearby levers, later replaced by those of a heavily weighted pattern.

With the increase of motor traffic on the Bristol to Weston-super-Mare road, the Weston Council thought fit to write a letter to the WCPLR on 17th November, 1932 saying that it was:

> not sufficient for the engine driver to blow a whistle, or make other signs to traffic which in these days, in spite of roadside notices, can hardly be expected to be prepared for a railway train to emerge suddenly from the side of the road and to cross one of the most extensively used roads in the West of England.

W. H. Austen, the manager, replied on 25th November saying that at the two points mentioned, the warning notices were illuminated, trains whistled and reduced speed to the statutory 8 mph. Trains were easily visible to road users:

> To have a flag or lamp at each level crossing as the council desired, would mean a delay of 5 minutes at each crossing and be resented by the travelling public. The company finds difficulty in competing with road traffic and compulsory stops would have a very serious effect on the undertaking.

Correspondence continued for a number of years, and on 3rd May, 1938 the Automatic Telephone & Electric Company installed traffic lights at the New Bristol Road and Locking Road East crossings. The green light was normally favourable to the road, but an approaching train operated a track treadle, manufactured by the Westinghouse Brake & Signal Company, sited 150 yds either side of the crossing. The depression of this treadle caused the road lights to change to amber, then red, the rail light changing to green. After a predetermined time the signals reverted to their original aspect. Once the treadle had been depressed, contacts were rendered inoperative for a period sufficiently long to ensure that the train could pass over the treadle on the far side of the crossing without causing the lights to change again. The light showed three aspects to road users and two to rail. Red was held for 90 seconds. Each set of apparatus cost £215 5s. 0d., the cost of installation being approximately £180 extra. Under an agreement dated 21st February, 1938, the Corporation of Weston-super-Mare defrayed the cost of £791 for sets of lights at both crossings. They were probably the first railway traffic lights in the country. Unfortunately children stepped on the treadle, or jammed it with a stone, holding up traffic when no train was about.

D. H. Robertson, an electrical contractor of 1 Chapel Hill, Clevedon was called in periodically to repair the telephone system. Austen realised it would be cheaper to employ him on a yearly contract of £10 from 1st October, 1934. He was required to visit each station at least once a Quarter to inspect the telephone and additionally was responsible for the general supervision of telephone lines throughout the system. When a fault was temporarily repaired by the company's staff, Robertson was required to solder the joints permanently. The telephone poles were so light that they were blown over by the wind, another hazard being stray cattle scratching themselves against them and pushing them over. Robertson stood on a coach roof to pull a pole erect, then jammed a stone into the enlarged hole to wedge it in position. In order to carry out his duties he was issued with a free pass. The company's telephones were on an omnibus circuit and he believes the code was:

5 bells for Portishead
4   „   „ Black Rock
3   „   „ Clevedon
2   „   „ Weston-super-Mare.

Note:

1. Drawing dated 13th September, 1920

A posed view of the 1872 Kitson built *Harold* on the opening day, 1st December, 1897. The engine was reported to have been painted in bright scarlet and carried the number 45 which was the owner's (Mackay & Davies of South Wales) own number. The traffic manager, E.R. Wintour stands on the ballast near the front of the engine, driver Jack Jones is on the footplate while George Hancock holds the rear buffer beam.   *L.G.R.P., courtesy David and Charles*

Clevedon standing at Weston-super-Mare in 1908. It will work bunker-first to Clevedon. Note how the paint has been removed by over-cleaning.
                                                                                     L.G.R.P., courtesy David and Charles

Chapter Eleven
Locomotives

The locomotive history of the WCPLR is somewhat confused, partly by the fact that names were transferred from one engine to another, and also because the company seems to have been very unskilful or very unlucky in its choice of engines. It appears that no locomotive had yet been delivered when the track was ready for test-runs and the first train of all was hauled behind a contractor's 0−4−0ST nicknamed 'Coffeepot' (a not unusual soubriquet for contractors' engines). As the company's 0−6−0T *Clevedon* was undergoing repair, the first public trains were probably worked by *Harold*, a Kitson 0−6−0T built 1872 for the contractor T. B. Nelson, bought in 1888 or 1889 by the Alexandra (Newport & South Wales) Docks & Railway for building its South Dock Extension for £450 and then sold to Mackay & Davies, this firm then hiring her to the WCPT. The number 45 as it appears on *Harold* when photographed on the WCPT is odd, the '4' being in the centre of the panel and the '5' an addition.

Another early engine was *Portishead*, a Robert Stephenson 0−6−0T built in 1880 and seemingly unused until 6th June, 1887 when she was sent to the Isle of Wight and used by the contractor William Jackson on his Freshwater, Yarmouth & Newport Railway contract, where she was named *Freshwater*. After working the first public trains, Jackson sold her to the London & St Katherine Dock Company. In October 1891 she was purchased by James and John Dickson, renamed *Longdown* after a local village, and used on their Exeter to Christow contract. In 1896−7 it returned to William Jackson and as *Portishead* he used it for working construction trains on the WCPT. It worked public trains for a period before being sold to the Renishaw Iron Company for £950 in April 1900. Withdrawn in 1937 it was probably scrapped in 1941.[1]

The Board of Trade returns for 30th June, 1898 show three engines in WCPT stock. These were probably the Walker 0−6−0T *Clevedon*, *Portishead* and *Harold*, a third engine being essential that month to be held spare when the increased service demanded two trains.

Clevedon, like *Portishead*, sported the legend 'WC&PT' painted prominently across its front buffer beam, proving that both certainly arrived before the company's change of name in June 1899. To ease running on the sharply curved transfer siding at Clevedon, they ran as 2−4−0Ts. *Clevedon*, a standard Walker engine for colliery use, was a neat machine with a short domeless boiler, raised fire box, full cab and bunker and originally supplied as *Bradford* with two others for T. A. Walker's Manchester Ship Canal contract. Bought by Jackson, the engine was bought by the WCPT when he gave up the contract in May 1897.

The company's next two locomotives were Sharp Stewart 2−2−2 well tank engines from the Furness Railway. The first named *Weston* was built in 1866 and the second, *Clevedon* in 1857. These outside-framed 'singles' were similar in most respects, but *Clevedon* had a full-width cab fitted by Avonside and a rectangular cast nameplate taken from the Walker engine of that name, while *Weston* had an oval engraved nameplate[2] on the side of the foremost boiler-ring, and a cab only the width of the firebox. Both had

The second locomotive to be named *Clevedon*, a 2–2–2T, seen here at Milton Road level crossing in the summer of 1898. Note the crossing gates, which were removed about a year later. The crew are William Preston (*left*) and Jack Jones (*right*). This was ex-Furness Railway No. 12A. *Author's Collection*

Weston near Wick St Lawrence in 1905. Driver George Hancock is on the footplate. *L.G.R.P., courtesy David and Charles*

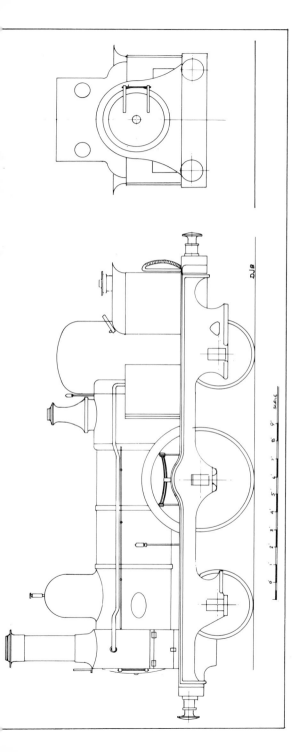

W.C.P.R. EX-FURNESS RAILWAY SHARP STEWART 2–2–2 No.1 WESTON

Traced by D.J. Burnett
Based on drawing by T. Coburn

A picture of Weston with its oval nameplate on the middle boiler position instead of the forward position (as in the drawing), seen here at Kingston Road, 1898.

G. Rushton Collection

The 2−4−0T, *Clevedon*, at Clevedon in November 1920. The Avonside plate is dated 1906. This engine arrived on the railway in 1901.

E.H. Hazell, courtesy J.J. Herd

The 0−6−0 locomotive *Weston* at Clevedon, April 1921. Note the large cab enclosing the bunker and the long nameplate replacing the original oval brass plate.

E.H. Hazell, courtesy J.J. Herd

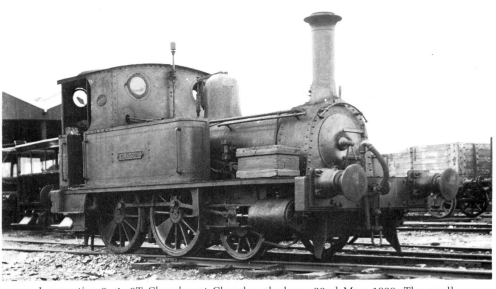

Locomotive 2−4−0T *Clevedon* at Clevedon sheds on 22nd May, 1929. The small railcar and trailer are on the left. This engine was reputedly the least powerful of the locomotive stud and used for the lightest of work.   *H.C. Casserley*

0−6−0, *Weston* at Clevedon. The cab's rear spectacle plate has been modified from the condition depicted on the opposite page so that the bunker is outside the cab. This was altered so that when the locomotive travelled in reverse, coal dust was less likely to blow into the crew's eyes.   *Photomatic Ltd*

'WC&P' in large capitals on the front buffer beam. They carried acetylene headlamps designed by Wintour which could 'brilliantly illuminate the track for 150 yards ahead.[3] *Weston* having larger cylinders, boiler and fire-box was more powerful than her sister and had brass, instead of iron tubes. On both engines, brake blocks operated on the driving and trailing wheels. *Clevedon* was probably scrapped at Clevedon in 1903 and *Weston* sold to the Bristol scrap dealer Joseph Pugsley in 1904 or 1905.

The next engine to arrive proved to be the company's longest serving locomotive, lasting until the line's closure. A 2−4−0T built by Dübs in 1879, named *General Don* she worked on the Jersey Railway. When that line was converted to 3 ft 6 in. gauge in 1884, she went as Curry & Reeve's contractor's locomotive to the North Cornwall Railway's Padstow extension. She arrived on the WCPLR in 1901 and worked still carrying her original name. In July 1906 she was fitted at Avonside Engine Works with vacuum brakes to allow her to work on passenger trains, a large cab replacing the 'cut-away' pattern. She also received a new boiler and cylinders. About this time the name-plates *Clevedon* from the 2−2−2WT were transferred to her. After breaking a connecting rod on the Yeo Bridge on 29th December, 1926 she lay dormant at the rear of No. 2 engine shed until repaired in 1936, when she was painted dark green with yellow letters and black and white lining. From then onwards she had to have an equalising trough to convey water to her far tank because the equalising pipe under the boiler was blocked. The box was placed across the boiler so that water could cross into the far tank, the equalising box then slung sideways on the boiler for travel. She could easily be identified by her very deep whistle. As *Clevedon* only blew 4 in. of vacuum instead of 21 in. the handbrakes had to be relied on. She was broken up at Swindon.

Emlyn No. 82 , a Kitson 0−6−0ST ran on the WCPLR on hire from Messrs C. D. Phillips of the Emlyn Engineering Works, Newport in 1902/5/6/7 to cope with the summer traffic. She ran with her rear pair of wheels un-coupled. The back of the cab was open to the elements, so it was just as well that she was not used in winter when cold winds howled across the flats. It bore a plate reading: 'Charles D. Phillips, Newport & Gloucester. Emlyn Engineering Works No. 1709'.

The next engine to be acquired was *Portishead*[4] a Sharp Stewart 2−4−0T of 1872 ordered by J. C. Craven for the Tunis & Goletta Railway, but then cancelled. Purchased by the LBSCR it became their No. 53 used on the West London Extension line until replaced by a 'Terrier'. Named *Bishopstone* it was used at Newhaven on harbour and breakwater works. Later as No. 270 *Fratton* it worked the Hayling Island branch and later still was No. 497. Sold to Cohen, the Nottingham scrap dealer in December 1890, she was resold to the WCPLR in 1903. The locomotive's distinguishing feature was the two pairs of windows at the front of the cab, the outer pair oval and the inner circular. Although withdrawn in 1906, she appeared on the WCPLR time-table poster for September 1907 (*reproduced on page 130*).

Emlyn No. 96 a Black, Hawthorn 0−6−0ST was hired in 1905 and was not fitted with a vacuum brake. The same year the WCPLR purchased an 1881

Manning Wardle class 'M' 0–6–0ST which it later named *Weston* using the
oval plates from the 2–2–2WT, later replaced by those of a cast iron pattern.
Originally built as the *Resolute* of J. M. Smith of Bury, it was sold a few years
later to Gabbutt & Owen of Huddersfield. The South Wales Anthracite
Company then purchased it for use at the Ynyscedwyn Colliery and in 1894
it went to the Burry Port & Gwendraeth Valley Railway to become their No. 7
Cwm Mawr. In August 1904 she was sent to Avonside Engine Works in part
exchange for a new engine with the same name and number, It varied from
most Manning Wardle saddle tanks in that it was fitted with an extended
saddle tank, flush at the front with the smoke box. It also had an enlarged
cab and first ran on the WCPLR with the rear pair of wheels uncoupled.
Peckett & Sons of Bristol rebuilt *Weston* in the early nineteen-twenties when
her red-brown livery was changed to apple green with red and yellow lining.
The rear spectacle plate was brought forward, placing the bunker outside,
instead of inside the cab, and three coal rails added. This modification made
coaling easier and helped prevent coal dust flying when working bunker
first. *Weston* was the best engine before the advent of the 'Terriers', and her
high pitched whistle could be instantly recognised and heard from afar
along the Gordano Valley. Latterly she was very run-down, W. E. Hayward
observing[5] *c.* 1937 'Without any exaggeration, the whole of *Weston* was "on
the joggle", cylinder blocks shifting in the frame and the smokebox, tank,
buffer beam and footplating were obviously loose in their bolts and rivets'.
She was scrapped in 1940 on site, not being taken to Swindon.

In 1907 with the opening of the Portishead extension imminent and only
the Dübs *Clevedon* and Manning Wardle *Weston* on the locomotive stock
list, another engine was urgently required. This was an 1890 Manning
Wardle 'K' class saddle tank. Its first owners, Logan & Hemingway of
Doncaster where she arrived on 21st April, 1890, used her as their No. 11 on
the Beighton and Chesterfield contract for the Manchester, Sheffield &
Lincolnshire Railway, where it shunted and tipped a record 400 wagons in a
single day. In 1898 it was sold to Naylor Brothers who used it on the contract
for Bunton–Parsly Hay and Ashbourne–Parsley Hay lines. It was bought
by Jackson & Company in 1900 who worked it on their Mid-Suffolk Light
Railway contract in 1902 and then on the Portishead contract. The WCPLR
purchased the engine and used it named *Portishead* for hauling the first
scheduled train over the extension. In 1926 she was sold to William Cowlin
& Son, Bristol for £125, being used on that firm's power station contract at
Portishead. When this was finished, she lay in a siding near the power
station at least until 1931 and although very rusty, much of her apple green
livery still showed.[6] Eventually she was sold to Joseph Pugsley for scrap.

On 4th June, 1908 a new and somewhat heavier 0–6–0ST named *Walton
Park* was delivered from Hudswell, Clarke & Company at a cost of £1200,
this being the company's first new engine. She was virtually a standard
contractor's locomotive with a few refinements for light railway passenger
working. The special fittings ordered were hand and vacuum brake, screw
couplings and a copper capped chimney and she was painted Midland red;
she was intended to work coal trains from Portishead. Unfortunately she
proved to be rather heavy for the road and was derailed on her first trip to

Locomotive 0–6–0ST *Walton Park* seen at Weston-super-Mare in 1908, painted Midland Red with copper chimney caps, just after delivery from Hudswell Clarke in Leeds.   *P. Strange Collection*

A shed line up of *Clevedon*, *Hesperus* and No. 5 at Clevedon on the 16th October, 1926. Notice water softener and tanks (*right*), and the spare rails in the foreground.
                                                                                                                   A.W. Croughton

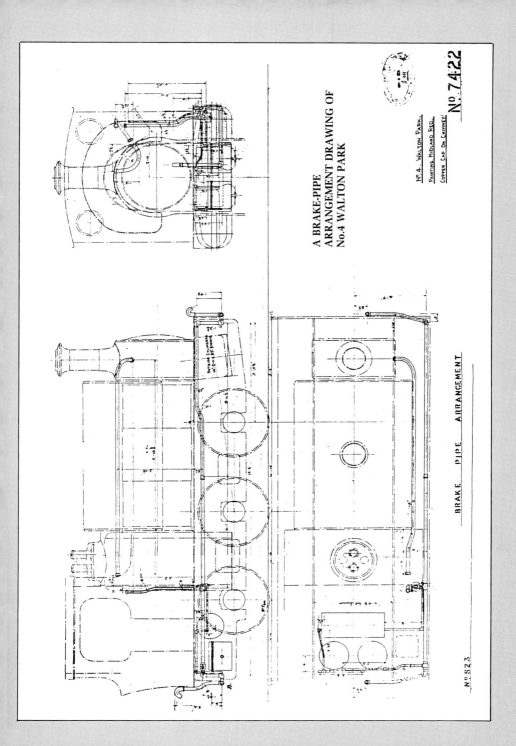

No. 74·22

A BRAKE-PIPE
ARRANGEMENT DRAWING OF
No.4 WALTON PARK

Nº 4. WALTON PARK.
PAINTING MIDLAND RED.
COPPER CAP ON CHIMNEY.

BRAKE PIPE ARRANGEMENT

Nº 823

Locomotive 0−6−0ST No. 5 at Clevedon, 13th July, 1935; with *Weston* (*left*) and *Hesperus* (*right*).   *S.W. Baker*

A side view of *Northiam* at Clevedon, November 1920. This engine was hired from the Kent and East Sussex Railway and appeared in the Will Hay film 'Oh, Mr Porter'.
E.H. Hazell, courtesy J.J. Herd

Weston-super-Mare. Little used after the autumn of 1909, she was transferred to another of Colonel Stephens' lines, the Plymouth, Devonport &
South Western Junction Railway in March 1912 and the following year to yet
another of his lines, the Shropshire & Montgomeryshire Light Railway. Later
it was sold to a further line in the Stephens' group, the East Kent Railway,
where it became their No. 2. They in turn sold it to T. W. Ward, Ilkeston in
1940. She was bought by the Purfleet Deep Wharf & Storage Company i
May 1947, who then named her *Churchill* and scrapped her in July 1957,
the last WCPLR engine to be broken up. Colonel Stephens, who arrived in
1911, numbered *Clevedon* 1; *Portishead* 2 and *Walton Park* 3, the latter
never actually receiving its number.

Walton Park proved too heavy for the WCPLR, and a replacement was
sought. This was No. 4 *Hesperus*, Stephens favouring classical names —
there being a 'Hesperus' also on the West Sussex, the Shropshire & Montgomeryshire and the Kent & East Sussex. Although, not counting loans, the
WCPLR had before 1910 bought nine engines, only four were added to stock
after that date. *Hesperus*, very similar to the 2−4−0T *Portishead*, was a
Sharp Stewart 2−4−0T built in 1876 for the Watlington & Princes Ris-
borough Railway. The line was bought by the GWR in 1883 and the engine
became GWR No. 1384. It was loaned to the Lambourn Valley when that line
opened in 1898. In 1899 it was rebuilt with a new boiler, Belpaire firebox
and cylinders and worked on the Wrington Vale Light Railway and then in
the Exeter and Laira districts. In April 1911 she was sold to the Bute Works
Supply Company, Cardiff, who resold it to the WCPLR. The 1384 plate was
removed in 1917 and she ran for a week without identification until the
name *Hesperus* was fitted.[7] About this date straps were fitted to secure the
cab roof. On 5th April, 1934 its weight broke a bridge on the Wick St
Lawrence Wharf line while working the branch when the Muir Hill tractor
was under repair. An ear-witness, Mr A. H. Parsons of Rose Farm, Wick St
Lawrence told a reporter: 'I was milking the cows two fields distant from the
line at 8 o'clock this morning when I heard a loud report and the sound of
cracking timber'. *Hesperus*, referred to colloquially as 'The Wreck' was little
used between then and it being sold as scrap for £40, and was cut up at
Clevedon in June 1937. Whilst on the Light Railway it always appeared to be
painted GWR green.

In August 1918 a Hawthorn, Leslie 2−4−0T No. 2 *Northiam* was lent by
the Kent & East Sussex Railway until 1920 as a temporary measure to relieve
a motive power shortage. She set out one Sunday morning from Rolvenden,
probably via Tonbridge, Redhill, Reading and Swindon, the driver booking
off 8.00 pm at Bristol, the journey being completed the next morning.[8] She
ran on the East Kent Railway from 1923 to 1930, and returned to the KESR to
receive fame when selected to star as *Gladstone* in the Will Hay film 'Oh, Mr
Porter' on location on the Southern Railway's Basingstoke & Alton Light
Railway in June 1937. She returned to the KESR and was scrapped in 1941.

A new Manning Wardle 0−6−0ST No. 5 arrived on 18th April, 1919. She
was of standard 'L' class appearance, apart from disc wheels to improve
adhesion, this modification causing the axleboxes to become so hot that
smoke or flames appeared. No. 5 was never repainted, just cleaned and

The unnamed 2—4—0T, *Hesperus* at Weston-super-Mare in 1911. George Newton is seen wearing his boater. Conductor W. Cullen stands on the right. *Author's Collection*

Now carrying its nameplate, *Hesperus* at Clevedon shed 13th July, 1935. Note the water softener in background and locomotive No. 5 (*left*). *S.W. Baker*

Locomotive 0−6−0ST *Portishead* at Portishead power station construction site in 1927. It had been sold to William Cowlin, Bristol, the previous year.

Photomatic Ltd

Left to right: Clevedon; Hesperus, with badly rusted smoke box; and the bunker of *Portishead*, all photographed at Clevedon shed on 22nd May, 1929.

H.C. Casserley

cleaned becoming almost black with age, yet really green, patches of the original colour still being visible in 1937.[9] She was sold in 1940, probably from Portishead, and not going to Swindon.

In 1926 the Manning Wardle saddle tank *Portishead* was replaced by an engine of the same name acquired from the Southern Railway. This engine had formerly been LBSCR No. 43 *Gipsyhill* built in June 1877. It had been renumbered 643 in 1902 and rebuilt with an extended smokebox at Brighton in August 1919. In 1920 she was experimentally equipped with the Angus automatic train control and worked light on trial over the Dyke branch with similarly equipped locomotive No. 680. On the WCPLR it retained its Westinghouse brake equipment and worked almost daily until 1936 when it went in to Clevedon shops for heavy repairs, which took two years to complete. Feedwater was pumped into *Portishead*, so it was impossible to fill the boiler when stationary. *Circa* 1938 *Portishead* was travelling from Walton Park towards Walton-in-Gordano with the LSW set, when the track spread causing one of the coaches to drop down. While waiting for the fitters from Clevedon to respond to the phone call, *Portishead* had to be uncoupled and run up and down to prevent the boiler running dry.[10] Taken over by the GWR in 1940, it was overhauled, the solid forged crank being replaced by a built-up crank; the boiler feed pumps which fouled the new cranks were replaced by standard GWR 8mm injectors; Westinghouse brake equipment was removed and a steam brake and GWR whistle and sight feed lubricators fitted. The LBSCR double lamp brackets giving a high or low lamp position were also removed. Painted green with a 'shirt button' totem, it still retained its nameplate. It was sent to St Philip's Marsh shed, Bristol and used on the Harbour lines and elsewhere, lasting long enough to become British Railways No. 5 in 1948. It shunted at Avonmouth in 1946 and by 1948 was at the engineers' depot, Taunton, and Dunball Wharf, going to Newton Abbot in January 1950, where it acted as shed pilot. Two months later it was sent to Swindon for storage. In 1953 the Bristol Railway Circle asked Weston-super-Mare Borough Council to preserve the locomotive as an attraction, but this suggestion was turned down in February as it could not afford the outlay of £400 and the engine passed to the scrap heap in March.

In 1936 and early 1937 the locomotive situation was desperate as the only engines available were *Hesperus* and No. 5: another was essential. The last engine to be acquired by the WCPLR was No. 4 which faced Portishead instead of Weston like most of the other locomotives. No. 4 was another ex-LBSCR 'Terrier'. Built in December 1875 as No. 53 *Ashtead* it was renumbered 653 in 1899 and rebuilt in 1912. For some time it had been wharf shunter at Littlehampton. As No. B653 it was withdrawn from service at Brighton in 1934 and placed in store at Eastleigh Works. In July the following year, it left after complete overhaul as No. 2653, the first 'Terrier' to receive the added 2000 to its number. The SR withdrew it from stock in February 1937, selling it to the WCPLR. It ran under its own steam to Salisbury, arriving on 11th February.

After spending the night there it continued the following morning still in charge of Southern enginemen, to Portishead. A maximum speed limit of 25 mph had been imposed, but this must have been interpreted with some

Locomotive *Clevedon* seen here at Clevedon in October 1937. Following an accident in 1926, this locomotive was taken out of service. It returned nine years later, in this livery. *R.G. Jarvis*

Portishead, also at Clevedon, 22nd May, 1929. *H.C. Casserley*

Locomotive No. 4 seen here at Clevedon in October 1937. This locomotive hauled the last public trains on the 18th May, 1940 and saw service with the GWR, when the line was taken over. *R.G. Jarvis*

LOCOMOTIVES OF THE WCPLR

No.	Wheel Arrangement	Name	Bldg Date	Maker	Maker's No.	Date Acq'd	Date W'drawn	
–	0–6–0T	Portishead	1887	R. Stephenson	2383	1898	1901	Ex-F.Y.N. contractors, IOW. Sold to Joseph Pugsley, Bristol. Ran as a 2–4–0T.
–	0–6–0T	Clevedon	1888	Walker Bros	–	1898	1899(?)	Ran as a 2–4–0T.
–	2–2–2WT	Weston	1866	Sharp Stewart	1707	1898	1904	Ex-Furness Rly No. 35A. Sold to Joseph Pugsley, Bristol.
–	2–2–2WT	Clevedon	1857	Sharp Stewart	1017	1899	1903	Ex-Furness Rly No. 12A. Scrapped at Clevedon 1906.
1	2–4–0T	Clevedon	1879	Dübs	1222	1901	1940	Built for Jersey Rly. Rebuilt Avonside 1906. Scrapped at Swindon 1940.
–	2–4–0T	Portishead	1872	Sharp Stewart	2242	1903	1906	Ex-LBSCR and Cohen.
3	0–6–0ST	Weston	1881	Manning Wardle	731	1906	1940	Ran as 0–4–2T on WCPLR. Ex Resolute J. M. Smith, Bury; Gabbutt & Owen, Huddersfield; Ynyscedwyn Colliery; Burry Port & Gwendraeth Valley Rly. Scrapped 1940.
(2)	0–6–0ST	Portishead	1890	Manning Wardle	1134	1907	1926	No. 11 Logan & Hemingway. Sold to Naylor Bros 1898. WCPLR sold it to William Cowlin, Bristol. Although numbered, not actually carried.
(4)	0–6–0ST	Walton Park	1908	Hudswell Clarke	823	1908	1912	To Plymouth, Devonport & South Western Jn Rly; Shropshire & Montgomeryshire Rly 1913; 1917 East Kent Rly No. 2; T. W. Ward, Ilkeston 1940; Purfleet Deep Wharf & Storage Co. 1947; scrapped 1957. Number 4 not actually carried.
(4)	2–4–0T	Hesperus	1876	Sharp Stewart	2578	1911	1937	Built for Watlington & Princes Risborough Rly; became GWR No. 1384. Scrapped 6/1937. Number 4 not actually carried.
5	0–6–0ST		1919	Manning Wardle	1970	1919	1940	Sold at closing.
2	0–6–0T	Portishead	1877	LBSCR	–	1925	1940	Ex-LBSCR No. 43 Gipsyhill, later No. 643. GWR No. 5, 1940. Withdrawn 1954.
4	0–6–0T		1875	LBSCR	–	1937	1940	Ex-LBSCR No. 53 Ashtead, later No. 653 and SR No. 2653. GWR No. 6, 1940. Withdrawn 1/1948.

HIRED LOCOMOTIVES

No.	Type	Name	Year	Builder	Works No.					Notes
45	0–6–0ST	Harold	1872	Kitson	1829	NA	NA	NA	NA	Hired from C. D. Phillips 1897/8
82	0–6–0ST	Emlyn	?	Kitson	?	NA	NA	NA	NA	Ran as 0–4–2T. Hired from C. D. Phillips for summers of 1902/5/6/7.
96	0–6–0ST	Emlyn	?	Black, Hawthorn	?	NA	NA	NA	NA	Hired from C. D. Phillips, summer 1905.
2	2–4–0T	Northiam	1899	Hawthorn, Leslie	2421	NA	NA	NA	NA	On loan from Kent & East Sussex Rly 1918–20.

DIMENSIONS OF WCPLR LOCOMOTIVES

No.	Builder	Locomotive name	Cylinders	Diameter coupled wheels	Boiler pressure lb./sq.in.	Heating surface sq.ft	Grate area sq.ft	Total wt tons
—	R. Stephenson	Portishead	14 in. × 18 in.	3 ft 6 in.	100	374	5¼	21
—	Walker Bros	Clevedon	13 in. × 20 in.	3 ft 3 in.	?	?	?	?
—	Sharp Stewart	Weston	15 in. × 18 in.	5 ft 7½ in.	?	176	9	25t 15 cwt
—	Sharp Stewart	Clevedon	14 in. × 18 in.	5 ft 7½ in.	?	136	9	23
1	Dübs	Clevedon	10 in. × 19 in.	4 ft	125	374	5¼	16⅛
1	Sharp Stewart	Portishead	12 in. × 17 in.	4 ft	140	570	7½	?
3	Manning Wardle	Weston	13 in. × 18 in.	2 ft 10½ in.	140	465	7¼	22
(2)	Manning Wardle	Portishead	12 in. × 17 in.	3 ft	140	366	7	16½
(4)	Hudswell Clarke	Walton Park	14 in. × 20 in.	3 ft 7 in.	170	560.29	8½	24
(4)	Sharp Stewart	Hesperus	12 in. × 17 in.	4 ft 2 in.	120	621	8½	24½
5	Manning Wardle	—	12 in. × 18 in.	3 ft 0½ in.	160	447	?	23½
2	LBSCR	Portishead	14 in. × 20 in.	4 ft	140	489	10	28¼
4	LBSCR	—	12 in. × 20 in.	4 ft	150	489	10	28¼

liberality, the engine arriving at Trowbridge 20 minutes early. Here the diminutive locomotive caused considerable amusement as the Southern authorities had chosen a driver of somewhat disproportionately ample dimensions to make the trip.[11]. No. 4 arrived at Clevedon beautifully tallowed with lines. 'Southern' and '2653' were painted out and replaced by its new initials and number 4. It had the honour of pulling the last passenger train over the Light Railway. In 1940 it was taken over by the GWR and given the number 6. Both 'Terriers' were given GWR Lot No. 342, Churchward and his successors extending the use of Lots to cover locomotives obtained from outside sources, even though the GWR had carried out no more than minor modifications. No. 6 was given a GWR whistle, but retained its vacuum and Westinghouse brakes and feed pumps. Both 'Terriers' were used in 1941 for the construction of the army depot's extensive sidings at Wapley Common, east of Westerleigh Junction on the Severn Tunnel to Wootton Bassett line.[12] Stationed at St Philip's Marsh, 1943 saw her loaned to the Ministry of Works for WCPLR track lifting, and she was once again stabled in Clevedon shed. Following this duty she was dispatched to Nottingham before being returned to Bristol. One of the 'Terriers' was loaned to Fry's chocolate factory, Keynsham, for a month or so when its Sentinel vertical boilered geared locomotive was undergoing repair. One of the 'Terriers' went down into the turntable pit at St Philip's Marsh. It had been moved here as it was useful for moving dead engines because it could draw a tank engine on to a turntable and remain with it, being so short.

Notes:

1. *A Locomotive History of Railways on the Isle of Wight*, D. L. Bradley
2. Probably engraved on the reversed FR number plate
3. *Railway Magazine*, June 1901, p. 526
4. J. H. P. Capell claims she was called *Clevedon*, though in photographs she is un-named
5. PRO: ZSPC 11/388
6. P. Strange
7. J. H. P. Capell
8. *Railways of Southern England: Independent & Light Railways*, E. Course
9. P. Strange
10. E. C. Carey
11. *Railway Magazine*, May 1937 p. 381
12. *St Philip's Marsh*, D. J. Fleming p. 60

Chapter Twelve

Internal Combustion Engined Stock

PASSENGER

Col Stephens was a pioneer of internal combustion engines for rail traction. As early as 1890 he arranged for an old Priestman oil engine to drive a tramcar bogie.[1] After World War I, owing to increased working costs and to avoid cutting services, the WCPLR made its first essay into internal combustion engined traction with a four-wheeled petrol railcar (Works No. 1252) purchased from the Drewry Car Company Ltd in October 1921. It was a most economical unit for the shuttle service between Clevedon and Weston. The water-cooled Baguley engine with radiator suspended below the buffer beam, had four cylinders with 4 in. bore and 5 in. stroke developing 25−30 hp at 1000 rpm. Power was transmitted through a three-speed gearbox by inverted tooth chain drive to one of the axles. Reverse also gave three-speeds and controls were fitted at both ends. The gears gave speeds of 5, 10 and 25 mph in either direction. Petrol consumption was 16 miles to the gallon and the average running and maintenance costs were only sixpence per train mile.

The bodywork consisted of three-ply wood panels covered with thin steel sheeting. Two doors either side at each end of the car gave access to the wooden slat seats placed each side of the gangway. The seat backs swung-over tramcar fashion to face the direction of travel. There was accommodation for 30 seated and 12 standing passengers. Steps below each door gave easy access from rail level. Weight in working order was six tons. The roof was railed round and a ladder at each end allowed luggage to be placed on it. The original three link couplings were soon changed for the screw variety.

The original acetylene lighting was replaced by electricity and a small headlight was also fitted at each end. The car's overall length measured 19 ft, it had a height of 8 ft 3 in. from rail level to the roof making it considerably lower than the company's coaches, and an extreme width of 8 ft. The handbrakes worked from either end and operated on the 2 ft diameter wheels placed outside the frames. These wheels bore the inscription 'British Griffin, Barrow, C&SLR' the initials presumably standing for the City & South London Railway. The original sidescreens were replaced by windows, all of which opened for ventilation, necessary as the fumes were overpowering at times, and for this reason regular passengers preferred riding in the trailer.

When new, the petrol tank was fitted inside the car body and it was usual to have as many as six full petrol cans underneath the rear seats, several, probably with missing caps. Eventually someone realised the potential danger as smoking was not prohibited. A cylindrical petrol tank was then fitted outside one end. The engine's exhaust pipe was carried up above roof level with a whistle hinged at its end. When the driver pulled a wire temporarily fitting it to the end of the exhaust it emitted a high-pitched warbling note, very similar to a British Telecom 'Trimphone'. The engine casing was in the car and the cooling water often boiled. If the radiator or filling vent cap was missing, the passengers were able to enjoy a Turkish bath *en route*. The railcar's livery was dark green relieved by yellow lining with the company's title in red fragile-looking letters on a gilt garter thinly

The small Drewry railcar leaving Clevedon for Portishead in the mid-1920s. Notice the 3-link coupling (not screw) and the ladder to give access to the roof which was railed round for luggage. Being powered by a water cooled 4 cylinder Baguley engine the vehicle carried a radiator below the buffer beam.   *A.H. Harbor Collection*

A 1927 view at Clevedon with the standard screw couplings and electric headlight now fitted. Notice the handbrake column inside the open door. The company garter decorates the side panel.   *Photomatic Ltd*

The small railcar and trailer seen here at Clevedon in the mid 1930s. Notice that the trailer has the glass windows which replaced the canvas drop curtains. The railcar view supports an extra large petrol tank on the front.   *M.E.J. Deane*

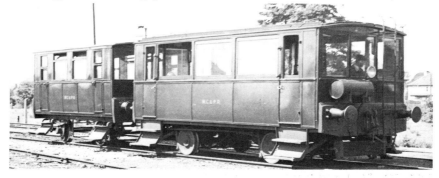

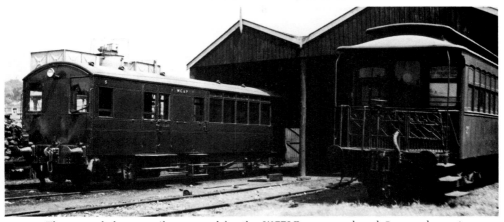

The second, larger, railcar owned by the WCPLR was numbered 5, seen here at Clevedon in July 1935. Built in 1928 by Drewry Car Company for the Southern Railway, it had capacity for 22 passengers and was purchased in 1934 for the railway. Its final resting place was as a sports pavilion at a Swindon girls' school.

S.W. Baker

The patterned moquette seating (red and black) of the interior of the large railcar. The seat backs could be moved so that passengers could sit facing the direction of travel. *Author's Collection*

The large railcar No. 5 seen here at Clevedon on 13th July, 1935. This view shows the radiator end of the vehicle. *S.W. Baker*

edged with red inside and out, placed on the side panel. The garter bore the legend 'Weston, Clevedon & Portishead Railway'. By 1937 the garter was replaced by the initials 'WC&PR' and the car number '1'. The first timetable for the railcar service was Monday, 12th June, 1922 and stated 'Motor rail car, one class only'. It was locally known as 'The Flying Matchbox' or the 'Dilly'.

All Saints' Church Sunday School, Clevedon went for an outing to Portishead in 'The Flying Matchbox'. All boarded at All Saints' halt, and because of the heavy load on the gradient, the car would not start. The children had to get out and then jump in when it was going.

When necessary a four-wheeled trailer was hauled. This was also supplied by the Drewry Car Company (Works No. 1323) and delivered on 23rd March, 1923. It seated 24 passengers and weighed 3 tons 5 cwts. Initially it was fitted with waterproof curtains instead of drop side windows, glass being fitted later. There were two, instead of three, end windows, and unlike the motor car it had outside axle boxes.

During the General Strike of 1926 the GWR arranged for the railcar and possibly its trailer, to run a morning and evening peak hour service on its Yatton branch. However the strike was settled before the Drewry and its crew was used. Stephens also ordered two locomotive crews to the GWR at Bath Road shed, Bristol.

A light four-wheeled wagon was supplied by Cranes (Dereham) Limited in September 1925 to carry extra luggage or the milk churns which were picked up at wayside halts. It had a capacity of 3 tons 10 cwt. The main frames were oak and the body measured 12 ft by 7 ft, with sides 18 inches deep and 1 inch thick. Hinged doors were fitted on each side. The steel disc wheels were 29 in. in diameter, a handbrake working on one pair. Screw couplings and side buffers were fitted, the latter having 'rectangular' faces with slightly curved ends.

In 1934 another four-wheeled Drewry car was bought, second-hand from the Southern Railway, their No. 5 built in 1928 (Works No. 1650). It seated 26 passengers and had a separate compartment for milk churns and luggage, taking up about half the body space. It had an electric headlight at both ends, the radiator protruding at the end opposite the brake portion. The wheelbase was 20 ft and the vehicle weighed 10 tons 17 cwt. It was used by the SR to work between Reading and Blackwater (Hants). Originally driven by a 50 hp engine (4¾ in. bore, 6 in. stroke), the three-speed gearbox gave maximum speeds of 8, 16 and 25 mph in either direction, the final drive being by inverted tooth chain. Circa 1933 it was fitted at Eastleigh with a Parsons M4 64 hp engine with 5 in. bore and 6 in. stroke. Four seats were removed to give an increased luggage capacity. Following this modification it worked Ashford–Appledore and New Romney–Dungeness, then Fareham–Gosport.

It arrived at Clevedon in the SR's standard dark olive livery with yellow and black lining. The cantrail bore the legend 'WC&P' in place of the words 'Southern Railway'. It retained its SR number, this being painted on the buffer beam some time after its arrival at Clevedon. This car sometimes pulled the low trailer built for railcar No. 1, its low roof line looking distinctly odd behind a car with a roof at the orthodox level. The proportion of passenger train miles run by railcars grew from 7612 (approximately a quarter) of the total passenger mileage in 1922, to 31,991 (about three-quarters) in 1938. Both railcars were periodically turned on the GWR table at Portishead to equalise flange wear. (The Metropolitan coaches and the LSW set were also turned c. 1925, but this was probably the only occasion.[2]) The railcars did not run on Wednesdays as George Morgan was both driver and mechanic and Wednesday was service day.

GOODS

In 1921 the WCPLR bought a Muir-Hill 'simple type conversion set' — a standard Fordson agricultural tractor fitted with special flanged dished wheels (40 in. in diameter) mounted directly on the tractor live-axle shaft. This was an ideal unit for the short workings at infrequent intervals as was required on the Wharf line. A special solid front axle was fitted with flanged wheels 24 in. in diameter. Buffing gear consisted of a channel iron frame of end and side members, supported on the rear axle housing at one end and on a cross-strut which rested on the forward end of the engine block at the other. Distance at the front end was kept by asbestos faced wood blocks fitted to the sides of the radiator. A simple cab was provided — just a roof supported on four uprights. The tractor weighed about 46 cwt, 35 cwt of this carried on the rear wheels and had a haulage capacity of 60 tons on the level.

Unfortunately within a year it came to a disastrous end. One wheel of this tractor had a tendency to revolve backwards when travelling at a certain speed.[3] At Kingston Road the guard looked out of his window on the service train towing the tractor from Wick St Lawrence to Clevedon sheds and saw that all he had on behind was the engine block. The tractor was, of course, damaged beyond repair.

As the machine had proved satisfactory, it was replaced in 1926 by a similar, though rather more elaborate tractor. This was also built by Muir-Hill Service Equipment Limited and was their No. A137. This again was basically a Fordson tractor with two solid chilled cast flanged wheels (40 in. in diameter) at the rear, but differed from the earlier model in having a solid front axle running in sprung axleboxes and also fitted with 40 in. diameter wheels. Substantial clamps on the rear axle housing attached a rectangular frame to the tractor, and was supported at the front end of the tractor by a cross member. The standard petrol-driven water-cooled engine had four cylinders with a bore of 4 in. and 5 in. stroke. The primary drive was to the rear wheels through the differential and standard Fordson rear axle casing. The front axle was turned by chain with sprockets fitted to the bosses on the rear wheels; sandboxes were also fitted. After delivery the WCPLR fitted the tractor with a glass panelled cab. Its weight was about 4 tons and it had a haulage capacity of around 75 tons on the level. Apart from shunting at the Wharf it was also used for powering the saw bench in the lean-to workshop on the side of the carriage shed. When taking on this role, it was run through the carriage shed, the track slewed to run the tractor to a special spur line. This shop was always busy patching up and bringing stock back into service. The tractor was scrapped when the railway closed.

The last internal combustion engined vehicle on the company's list was a troublesome Fairmont petrol-engined gangers' motor trolley used for permanent way inspection. Additionally there were two velocipedes and five pump trolleys but the latter could not be started by pumping the handles, the drive crank requiring to be pushed and then when in motion one could jump on and start pumping, reaching a maximum speed of about 20 mph. There was a footbrake between two of the wheels. In the nineteen-thirties one pump trolley was stored beside the track between Ham Lane and the Yeo Bridge, a chain being put through its wheels and locked. One link of the chain had a spring link like a large key ring and could be eased open with a screw driver as youths discovered and, after taking a joy ride one Sunday, left the trolley in a ditch.

Notes:

1. *The Locomotive*, 15th September, 1922 p. 253
2. E. C. Carey
3. *Ibid*

The second rail tractor purchased from Muir-Hill in 1926. The chassis had 40 inch flanged wheels and had the hauling capacity of over 70 tons (note the sandboxes). The fitting shops at Clevedon equipped the chassis with its wooden and glass body.

L.G.R.P., courtesy David and Charles

Chapter Thirteen

Coaching & Goods Stock and Liveries

The first coaches, or cars as they were called in tramway parlance, were bought from the Lancaster Railway Carriage & Wagon Company Ltd and originally destined for the Argentine Republic Railway. This contract fell through, probably at an early stage, as the axle boxes had the cast inscription 'Weston & Clevedon Tramways'. The six cars were of typical American pattern with observation platforms at each end and indeed were ideal for a railway with either low, or no platforms at the stations. They had centre gangways, straight sides and clerestory roofs. Ventilators were added and the clerestory windows subsequently painted, to save keeping them clean. The bodies were entirely mahogany and made in sections held together by brass screws for easy 'knocking down' for shipping. There was wrought iron work at the end of the platforms and gates on the ends as well as the sides so that the conductor could pass from car to car to issue tickets. A notice on each end read: 'Passengers are not allowed to ride on car platform'. The cars dimensions were:

Length over buffers	49	ft	3 in.
Length of body	39	ft	9 in.
Width of body	7	ft	9 in.
Height from rail level	12	ft	5 in.
Weight	8½ tons		

Chain brakes were fitted, applied by the guard on the front platform of the first coach. In the event of an emergency, a driver sounded three pips on the whistle, the conductor applying the brakes on the second coach if there was one. Before the introduction of the vacuum brake in July 1899, side chains were used to guard against breakaways. Later, perhaps during World War I, the duties of the conductor and guard were combined to save manpower. Spoked wheels were in frail-looking diamond bogie frames fitted with spiral springs. A chain was fitted to restrict movement of a derailed bogie.

On trial trips, reporters remarked on the free running of the cars and the complete freedom from oscillation. After 1899 'Weston Clevedon & Portishead Railway Company' was written above the windows, which lifted open instead of dropping as was normal British practice. There were two classes of accommodation and the seats were arranged[1]:

Coach No.	1st class	2nd class
1	10	45
2	10	35
3	10	42
4	10	35
5	10	35
6	10	42

The original seating was arranged longitudinally as in a tramcar, though seats were lateral beyond the draped curtains separating the first class section. First class seats were upholstered in dark, almost black, rexine, and sprung, second class passengers having to sit on American bent wood. During the winter of 1900–1 the second class seats of at least one car were

The 'American' coaches of the WC&PT. These six coaches arrived at Clevedon in pieces and were assembled in the workshops. Originally built for the Argentine Railway by the Lancaster Railway Carriage and Wagon Co Ltd, they were made completely of mahogany with wrought ironwork and gates at the end of each vehicle.

Coach No. 6 at Clevedon, 1921.   *E.H. Hazell, courtesy J.J. Herd*

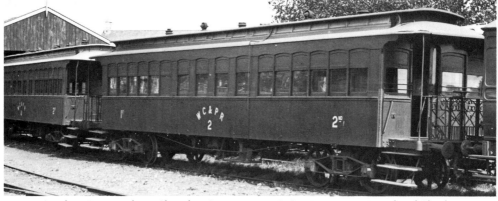

Coaches Nos. 2 and 4 at Clevedon, June 1937.   *L.G.R.P., courtesy David and Charles*

The interior of coach No. 2 seen here at Swindon on the 21st August, 1940. This coach was lit by acetylene gas, and is reputed to have been the first vehicle in the country to be so equipped.   *British Rail*

arranged transversely and then seated 50 to 60 second class passengers and 10 first. The tramcar atmosphere was increased by advertisements above the windows and under the longitudinal luggage racks. In early days, some cars carried a white label bearing the letters 'SMOKING', this also being displayed on some windows.

The cars were originally lit by lamps burning mineral oil, but these gave a poor light and E. R. Wintour, pleased with acetylene lighting on the loco-motives, provided an apparatus which was slung underneath the cars for generating acetylene gas. In fact it was the first railway in Great Britain to adopt acetylene gas as a standard lighting system.

Two or three of these cars formed a train, but by 1929 they had fallen from favour, having the disadvantage that smoke from the engine often used to descend and blow through the open end of the second or third coach. Regular passengers learnt by experience to use the front coach. Cars Nos. 3, 5 and 6 were sold in 1935, half of one body being used as a hut at Clevedon in Fitter Hill's garden, while Nos. 1, 2 and 4 were painted dark green, including the upper part of the windows, to match the railcars, with 'WC&PR' in an arc, the car's number set below in the same style as the locomotives. They were useful for Sunday School outings and other group parties as passengers could travel together. Many a lad stood on the end platforms and in imagin-ation 'pumped lead' into pursuing redskins or cattle-rustlers. After closure the three cars were taken to Swindon for scrapping or sale, one being used as a cabin in the wagon works there until broken up in 1954.

Coach No. 7 was an ex-Great Central Railway open vehicle purchased c.1901. Known as the 'charabanc' it was used only occasionally to provide emergency accommodation, benches being placed on it. In 1913 it was renumbered 13 in the goods list and left in the former passing loop at Wick St Lawrence where it rotted away.

With the opening of the extension to Portishead, more rolling stock was needed. The company managed to purchase seven compartment vehicles built by Craven's Railway Carriage & Wagon Company in 1870 for the Metropolitan Railway and made redundant by electrification. The WCPLR numbered them 8 to 14. Built specially to the Metropolitan design, except for No. 14 (later No. 7 an open saloon) they were in two sets of close-coupled triplets, later arranged in close-coupled twin sets Nos. 8 & 13; 9 & 10; 11 & 12, each pair measuring 43 ft 8 in. in length. The compartments were 7 ft 1 in. high internally. The straight-sided doors had half-round tops so that if left open they would not foul tunnel walls. Bars across the windows prevented passengers leaning out in tunnels to their disadvantage. The wheels were spoked. The *Clevedon Mercury*[2] enthused:

> With the development of the train service between Clevedon, Portishead and Weston-super-Mare by the Light Railway more rolling stock became necessary, and this was brought into use for the first time on Monday, (2nd September), when some of the trains were made up of carriages which have recently been secured. Those who journey by them could not fail to have marked their easy running and comfortable accommodation, and possibly some of the passengers recognised in the coaches some old friends which used to run on the Metropolitan Railway before that system was electrified. However, their use on the Light Railway is to be

The ex-LSWR set of 3 coaches purchased from the Southern Railway. Numbered 15, 16 and 17 by the WCPLR, the coaches normally ran as a triple set but occasionally with the centre coach omitted. They were steam heated and electrically lit by a dynamo on coach No. 15. Photographed at Clevedon on the 13th July, 1935.

S.W. Baker

Ex-Great Eastern railway brake van, No. 14 at Clevedon, in June 1937 believed to have been purchased 1911 and used mainly for the transport of milk churns.

L.G.R.P., courtesy David and Charles

Ex-Metropolitan Railway coaches. Nos. 8 (*left*) and 13 at Weston-super-Mare, August 1937. *L.G.R.P., courtesy David and Charles*

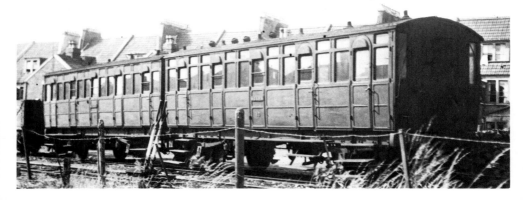

welcomed, if only as a change from the other carriages, which are open all down the centre, and in which travellers sit sideways, as it were, and not in the way usual in ordinary railway carriages. The new carriages are corridors, and give the officials communication right through the trains, which are made up of three coaches. The outsides are painted in what is known as 'Midland Red' and inside the first-class compartments are upholstered in red plush. The only other class is second and here the seats and rests are upholstered in tapestry. The lighting is by Pintoch's[3] [sic] patent gas, the same as on other railways, and so doing away with the acetylene gas. There are luggage racks and every convenience for passengers, the doors automatically locking themselves. The new stock also contains good accommodation for the guards, with two powerful hand breaks [sic] in addition to the vacuum brake on the engine. The seven extra coaches make fourteen altogether, three trains being employed in running backwards and forwards throughout the day, with no Sunday service.

The provision of the new carriages shows commendable enterprise on the part of the company, and is bound to render the line even more popular for traffic in the future than it has been in the past. The staff working the trains are also in neat uniforms, and are unfailing in their courtesy towards passengers.

The coaches were fitted with steps for access at halts without platforms and, even with this help, climbing in for the less athletic was quite an undertaking. There were doors, or side corridors, between each compartment and end doors and footplates between the coaches in each close-coupled pair. Later on the second class seats were upholstered in red leather, moquette or just plain wood. First class passengers enjoyed the luxury of leather-covered seats. In the nineteen-thirties the seating and interior of these coaches was still of good quality.[4] No. 14 was a former four compartment first with an overall length of 27 ft 6 in. and Nos. 8 to 13, originally in two sets of three, were in three close-coupled sets; two with five compartments to each coach and one with five compartments and four compartments respectively. One end compartment in each set was converted for guard's use. When the ex-GER coach was renumbered, the vacant No. 7 was filled by No. 14.

A tailoring firm purchased all the ex-WCPLR four-wheeled coaches from the GWR at Swindon and set them up as military tailoring shops in various camps between Shrivenham and Watchfield a few miles east of Swindon. No. 7 ended as an antique shop at Shrivenham still with '7' on its side and with original ceiling, a luggage rack and one seat. It is now in the London Transport collection, but at the time of writing has yet to be restored.

No. 14 was a four-wheel passenger brake van purchased from the Great Eastern Railway in 1916. After being overturned in a shunting accident in 1927 with 40 churns on board, its frames were twisted and it never ran again, although at a cursory glance appearing quite sound.

Three ex-LSWR four-wheel coaches were bought from the Southern Railway, one in 1925 and two in 1926 and were close-coupled as a three-coach set, though sometimes running with the middle coach missing. It formed the favourite train in the 'thirties. There were doors between the compartments and also between the coaches so that the conductor could pass along the train. The first class seats were upholstered in blue cloth and the second in red and black moquette.

No. 15 had a central saloon for second class passengers, a first class saloon at one end and a second class and a guard's compartment at the other; No. 16 had five second class compartments, while No. 17 had two second class compartments and one second class compartment either side of a central second class saloon. The guard's compartment in No. 17 had a dynamo to light the set which was steam heated. Like the Metropolitan coaches, steps were fitted for ground access.

No. 18 was a four-wheeled ex-Taff Vale second class passenger brake purchased from the GWR in 1928 to replace the GER full brake damaged in the mishap. Between two second class compartments and the luggage compartment was the guard's section with distinctive duckets.

The vacuum brake was fitted to all passenger stock and locomotives had the usual large and small ejectors, yet coach and engine handbrakes were used rather than the vacuum brake even though this was coupled up, the object being to save steam.

The 28 wagons and vans owned by the WCPLR were used for internal traffic only, mostly consisting of 6-ton low-sided and 8- and 10-ton open wagons and one covered cement truck. Until the opening of the Portishead extension in 1907 the company only possessed 3 wagons, but to cope with the additional traffic another 6 were obtained with another 9 arriving the following year. Six more came in 1922. No. 17 was a six-wheeled trolley wagon with a very shallow well and an ex-Midland Railway brake van completed the stock. The well wagon was stored for years at Wick St Lawrence, then sent to the Shropshire & Montgomeryshire Railway together with 3 three-plank dropside wagons, being carried beyond Portishead in Great Western well wagons, all this stock eventually returning to the WCPLR. The box van was last used in 1932 as a mobile carpenter's workshop when Milton Road shelter was built. There were very rarely any goods which needed to be loaded into a van. Wagon No. 19 was used as a trailer for the small Drewry before the special milk wagon was purchased, stanchions being fitted on the sides to rest on a milk platform and prevent the side dropping right down. The MR brake van was used on the 3.30 pm Clevedon to Portishead freight working until 1924, any passengers riding in the van on long seats.[5] The van was not used after this date. At closure 27 open wagons and 1 van were recorded.

Some 65,000–70,000 tons of stone per annum comprised the principal traffic, but there was also a considerable carriage of coal, milk and some timber. Private owners' wagons seen on the line included: Renwick Wilton & Co. Ltd; Radstock Coal Co.; Kilmersdon Colliery, Radstock; Baldwin (Bristol); Mapperley Colliery; Rose, Smith & Co. Ltd; William Butler; Stephenson Clarke.[6] Other wagons remembered were: Bolsover, Butterley, G.L.M., Tirpentwys, Crutchley's, Burnham, and Gilman.[7]

COMPANY LIVERY

Most station buildings were painted buff with white window and door frames and red oxide roofs. Portishead was creosoted black as was Walton Park.

In the early years, engines and coaches were a dark crimson with black and vermilion linings and locomotives had copper-capped chimneys and brass domes, with 'WC&PT' painted on the buffer beams. Bill Cullen was a conductor in the summer and a painter in the winter. When George Newton left, he gave all the paint to him. Under the management of Colonel Stephens, Cullen painted the engines and coaches under contract. The paint used was 'Mercedes Red' manufactured by Docker Brothers of Birmingham. It is believed that no coaches or locomotives were painted brown, this colour being merely weathered maroon.[8]

By 1927 most of the engines were green (*Hesperus* keeping her GWR green, the others being a lighter shade), the *Railway Magazine* of January 1938 recording that *Clevedon* and No. 4 had been painted a 'bright green'. In actual fact, No. 4 retained her Southern green, only the tank panel being repainted to cover the Southern lettering and number to be replaced by that of the WCPLR. In the mid-thirties coaches Nos. 1, 2, 4 and 18 were painted unlined mid green, the paint being purchased locally at Clevedon by carpenter and painter Jack Ralph. The LSW coaches had their roofs painted white in 1939, the supply running out when the task was partly completed, the coaches still running in service in this condition and looking odd. Latterly the LSW coaches were always a reddish brown colour and the Metropolitan coaches varnished mahogany giving a rich red colour. The ends of the LSW and Metropolitan sets were painted red, though faded to a pink hue.[9]

In the 'thirties livery coaches and locomotives Nos. 1 and 4 had the letters WC&PR set in an arc, with the coach or engine number below. On coaches this was in white, while on locomotives it was yellow. The number of the locomotive was painted on the red buffer beam in white. Until this new livery was introduced, coaches bore a cast plate with the legend 'WC&PR', another bearing its number. The small Drewry at first bore the company's garter, 10 in. by 11 in. replaced later by straight lettering. Both rail cars were painted dark green.

The goods stock vehicles were grey with white lettering and the brake van carried a cast plate.

Notes:

1. *Railway Magazine*, June 1938 p. 421
2. *Clevedon Mercury*, 7th September, 1907
3. This lighting system was introduced into Prussia by Julius Pintsch. It used a mixture of 20% acetylene and 80% oil or coal gas, producing optimum illumination with minimum risk.
4. A. H. Harbor
5. Howard Carey
6. Dick Kelham
7. Howard Carey
8. E. C. Carey
9. *Ibid*

Locomotive No. 4 heading a mixed train from Clevedon to Portishead, consisting of coach No. 18, tar wagon and a GWR open wagon, seen here crossing Walton Road in December 1937. *P. Strange*

Locomotive *Portishead* seen here at Weston-super-Mare, *c.*1908 with a WCPLR open wagon as tail traffic. *L.G.R.P., courtesy David and Charles*

Driver Tom Gatford pressing locomotive No. 4, seen here passing Broadstone with the LSWR set in June 1938. Notice the flimsy fence and lack of earthworks with the track on concrete sleeper blocks. The land on the left was acquired for possible sidings. *L.G.R.P., courtesy David and Charles*

Chapter Fourteen

Timetables and Train Working

The WCPT opened on the 1st December, 1897 with 5 trains each way and an additional evening working on Wednesdays and Saturdays; they took 45 minutes for the journey. (It was deemed 'down' from Clevedon to Weston.) The New Year saw the timetable modified in the light of experience, all afternoon timings being 15 minutes later, the final train on Wednesdays, Thursdays and Saturdays 30 minutes later. Brown's omnibus service gave a connection to and from Portishead, through booking being also available. From 21st February, 1898 a bus met all trains at Weston-super-Mare and ran to the High Street. On 30th April two extra trains ran daily, making a total of 7, plus 1 on Saturdays and a Sunday service was introduced with a service of 3 each way. The month of June saw the weekday service extended to 12 trains each way; the 45 minute frequency in the afternoon requiring the use of two trains and the passing loop at Wick St Lawrence. The crew of the first train worked from 8 am–7.30 pm, the second crew working from 1.45 pm–11 pm, changing turns each week and working alternate Sundays. It is interesting to note that 16 trains were run on August Bank Holiday Monday. The winter service (starting in November) showed 6 trains each way plus a late train on Saturdays. The pattern was:

November to March — 6 return journeys
April, May, and October — 8 return journeys
June to September — 12 return journeys.

E. R. Wintour, the energetic traffic manager, sought traffic with special trains and cheap fares. So in 1900 he issued market tickets on Tuesdays to Weston-super-Mare by four morning trains at single fare for the return journey from all stations except Milton Road. In September special late trains were run in connection with Worle's Harvest Festival celebrations and specials were run to and from the Guy Fawke's Carnival at Weston-super-Mare. Extra services were run for any special event and also on Bank Holidays, the latter stretching the line's resources to the full, three trains being run and the company's entire staff engaged helping the traffic department. Wintour saw that the press was kept informed, the *Clevedon Mercury* of 2nd July, 1898 carrying the news item: 'Visitors to Clevedon should not fail to make a trip to Weston by the new steam tramway. Haymaking is now in full swing either side of the line, and the run is most enjoyable. The return fare is only one shilling'. In September 1900 the slant was: 'For blackberrying, book to Ham Lane or Wick St Lawrence. The blackberries are now ripe and very plentiful'.

An innovation in May 1902 was the introduction of limited stop trains, though scheduled times were the same as those of all-stations services. Brown's horse bus advertisements now had the additional words 'No connection with the cars', for Richard Stephens who lived in Clevedon and claimed to have designed and built the first entirely English motor car, also built the first motor bus. From at least as early as 1903 this 12 hp vehicle could carry 9 passengers and ran from Clevedon to Portishead in connection with trains. Both Brown and Stephens ceased running when the WCPLR service was opened to Portishead.

| **May & June.** | | | **TIME TABLE.** | | | | | | | | | | **1905.** |

			Week-days										**Sundays.**
	a.m		a.m		a.m|p.m	p.m|p.m		p.m|p.m	p.m	p.m	p.m	p.m	
Clevedon dep	8 15	...	10 0	...	1130|1255	2 5|4 15	5 55|7 15	8 8 35|9		0 10s25	No
Colehouse Lane,,	8 18	...	10 3	...	1153	...	2 18|4 18	5 58|7 18	8 8 38|9		3 10s28	
Kingston Road ,,	8 21	...	10 6	...	1136	...	2 21|4 21	6 1|7 21	8 8 41|9		6 10s31	Sunday
Ham Lane ,,	8 24	...	10 9	...	1139	...	2 24|4 24	6 4|7 24	8 8 44|9		9 10s34	
Wick St. Lawrence	8 28	...	1013	...	1143	6 2 28	4 28	6 8	7 28	8 8 48	9		13 10s38	
Ebdon Lane ,,	8 31	...	1016	...	1146	9 2 31	4 31	6 11	7 31	8 8 51	9		16 10s41	Trains.
Worle ,,	8 36	...	1021	...	1151	13 2 36	4 36	6 16	7 36	8 8 56	9		21 10s46	
Milton Road ,,	8 41	...	1026	...	1156	2 41	4 41	6 21	7 41	9 9 1	9		26 10s51	
Weston-s-Mare arr	8 45	...	1030	...	12 0	20 2 45	4 45	6 25	7 45	9 8 5	9		30 10s55	
Weston-s-Mare dep	9 0	...	1045	...	1215	30 3 0	5 0	6 35	7 55	9 8 15	9		45 11s 5	No
Milton Road ,,	9 3	...	1048	...	1218	33 3 3	5 3	6 38	7 58	9 8 18	9		48 11s 8	
Worle ,,	9 7	...	1052	...	1222	37 3 7	5 7	6 42	8 2	9 8 22	9		52 11s12	
Ebdon Lane ,,	9 11	...	1056	...	1226	41 3 11	5 11	6 46	8 6	9 8 26	9		56 11s16	Sunday
Wick St. Lawrence	9 14	...	1059	...	1229	44 3 14	5 14	6 49	8 9	9 8 29	9		59 11s19	
Ham Lane ,,	9 18	...	11 3	...	1233	48 3 18	5 18	6 53	8 13	9 8 33	10		3 11s23	
Kingston Road ,,	9 22	...	11 7	...	1237	52 3 22	5 22	6 57	8 17	9 8 37	10		7 11s27	Trains.
Colehouse Lane,,	9 26	...	1111	...	1241	56 3 26	5 26	7 1	8 21	9 8 41	10		11 11s31	
Clevedon arr.	9 30	...	1115	...	1245	2 0 3 30	5 30	7 5	8 25	9 8 45	10		15 11s35	

s Saturdays only.

Brown's Bus or Char-a-Banc.   Return Fare, 2nd Class, Weston & Portishead, 2/-

Clevedon dep.	11.55	3.30	7 30	Portishead, dep.	10.20	12.55	5.0
Portishead arr.	12.40	4.15	8.15	Clevedon arr	11.5	1.10	5.15

RETURN FARES, Weston & Clevedon, 1s. (2nd Class).

Stephen's Motor Cars.   Return Fare, Clevedon and Portishead, 1s. 6d.

Clevedon dep.	9.40	11.55	3.30	5.30	7.45	Portishead dep.	10.20	12.55	4.0	6.0	8.15
Portishead arr.	10.10	12.25	4.0	6.0	8.15	Clevedon arr.	10.50	1 35	4 30	6. 7	8.50

FARES.

Weston to Milton, (2nd Class) Single—1d.		(1st Class) Single—1½d.		
,,	Worle	,,	2d.	,,	3d.	Return Tickets
,,	Ebdon	,,	3d.	,,	4½d.	are NOT
,,	Wick	,,	4d.	,,	6d.	issued to
,,	Ham Lane	,,	5d.	,,	7½d.	intermediate
,,	Kingston	,,	6d.	,,	9d.	stations.
,,	Colehouse	,,	7d.	,,	10½d.	
,,	Clevedon	,,	8d.	,,	1/-	
,,	,, (2nd Class) Return 1/-		(1st Class) Return	1/6		

Clevedon to Coleh'se (2nd Cl.) Single—1d.		(1st Cl.)	e—1½d.		
,,	Kingston	,,	2d.	,,	3d.	Return Tickets
,,	Ham Lane	,,	3d.	,,	4½d.	are NOT
,,	Wick	,,	4d.	,,	6d.	issued to
,,	Ebdon	,,	5d.	,,	7½d.	intermediate
,,	Worle	,,	6d.	,,	9d.	stations.
,,	Milton	,,	7d.	,,	10½d.	
,,	Weston	,,	8d.	,,	1/-	
,,	,, (2nd Class) Return, 1/-		(1st Class) Return, 1/6		

Weston and Clevedon Light Railway.

The Popular and most Direct Route between Weston-super-Mare and Clevedon. Largely used by Cyclists. The distance between the above Towns is only **Eight Miles** (by road it is fifteen miles). The Charge for Cycles accompanied by passengers) is **4d.** for the whole or any distance. Passengers alighting at Worle should not fail to visit Woodspring Priory.

PARKER'S RESTAURANT (Worle), 3 minutes from Light Railway.

The 1905 Summer timetable.

An ill wind blew to some good on 10th September, 1903 when a storm damaged Weston-super-Mare pier so badly that paddle steamers could not use it. Boats carried Cardiff passengers to Clevedon where they caught the Light Railway to Weston this arrangement continuing until the end of the year. A circular tour from South Wales was quite a feature, excursionists travelling by paddle steamer to Weston, the Light Railway to Clevedon where they lunched at the Bristol Hotel, Chapel Hill; then transport to Clevedon pier and back by sea to South Wales. On one rather more recent occasion a steamer from Ilfracombe was late, consequently missing the tide at Weston. The quick-thinking captain realised he would just catch the tide at Clevedon, so landed Weston passengers there, where they made their way to the WCPLR station. Too many for the Drewry railcar, luckily one of the 'Terriers' was just in steam. Pressure was raised, it was then coupled to the ex-LSWR set and drew the large number of passengers to Weston-super-Mare.

With the opening to Portishead in 1907, the September timetable showed 8 trains each way on the Portishead section (through to and from Weston-super-Mare) plus a late train on Wednesdays and Saturdays Weston–Portishead, returning to Clevedon as Empty Coaching Stock. Timing varied between 25 and 30 minutes for the run. Fourteen trains were shown on the Weston-super-Mare section plus one late train on Wednesdays and Saturdays: 25–30 minutes were allowed on this section and about an hour from Weston to Portishead. Most trains continued to cross at Wick St Lawrence rather than Clevedon, in fact for trains to cross at Clevedon, one had to be scheduled to depart 5 minutes before the other, to allow for the earlier one to do its work and run into the loop before the arrival of the other. Wick continued to be a passing place until 1914.

The *Clevedon Mercury*[1] noted:

> A frequent and convenient service of trains is run, and the excursions arranged on Thursdays from Portishead to Weston-super-Mare and back for a shilling are very well patronised. This gives a 28 mile run, and for an extra 4d. the entertainments, afternoon or evening, on the Grand Pier, can be visited. There were also cheap excursions on Wednesdays from Clevedon to Portishead or Weston, at the return fare of 6d., giving equal amusement facilities at the latter town, besides which special excursions are frequently announced.

The winter timetable 1907–8 showed 8 trains on the southern section and 6 on the northern section. The first train from the carriage shed ran services from 7.45 am–4 pm and the second 3.30 pm–10 pm. In summer there were 13 and 7 trains on the respective section. July 1908 saw the resumption of Sunday services after a break of 4 years.

The Portishead extension did not prove as profitable as anticipated and services were gradually decreased, November 1915 seeing the worst service offered by the WCPLR, 3 trains serving Portishead and 4 to Weston. With the placing into service of the internal combustion engine railcar on 12th June, 1922, most Clevedon to Weston trips were worked by this economical vehicle, its introduction allowing a more frequent service of 8 trains on the southern section, a year later this being increased to 11. A steam engine still continued to work most Clevedon to Portishead trains as the majority of

WESTON, CLEVEDON, AND
PORTISHEAD

Light

Railway

TIME TABLE.

SEPTEMBER, 1907.

Down Trains. **WEEK DAYS.**

		a.m.	a.m.	a.m.	a.m.	p.m.	p.m.	p.m.	p.m.	p.m.	p.m.	p.m.	p.m.	p.m.	p.m.	p.m.	p.m.
Portishead	dep.	9 w	0	10 5			12 20		2 17		4 0		5 30		7 w30	9 30	
Portishead South	,,	9	4	10 8			12 23		2 20		4 5		5 35		7 33	9 35	
(Purtbury Road)																	
Clapton Road	,,	9	6	10 10			12 26		2 23		4 8		5 38		7 36	9 40	
Cadbury Road	,,	9	11	10 13			12 29		2 26		4 15		5 45		7 39	9 49	
(Weston-in-Gordano)																	
Walton-in-Gordano	,,	9	16	10 15			12 33		2 30		4 20		5 50		7 43	9 52	
Walton Park	,,	9	18	10 17			12 36		2 33		4 26		5 55		7 46	9 57	
Clevedon East	,,	9	22	10 20			12 40		2 37		4 30		6 0		7 50	10 2	
Clevedon	,,	8 w59	35	10 30	11 10	12 25	1	0 2	1 52	2 47	3	4 25	2 26 w	157	30 8	7 10	7 10* 15
Colehouse Lane	,,	8 7w	38	10 33	11 13	12 27		2 17	2 50	3 04	4 55	2 56	187	328	10	
Kingston Road	,,	8 10w	41	10 36	11 16	12 30		2 20	2 53	3 34	4 85	2 86	217	358	13	
Ham Lane	,,	8 13w	44	10 39	11 19	12 33		2 23	2 56	3 64	4 15	3 16	247	388	16	
Wick St. Lawrence	,,	8 16w	48	10 43	11 23	12 36	11 2	2 63	0 3	4 04	5 55	3 56	287	418	20	
Ebdon Lane	,,	8 19w	51	10 46	11 26	12 39		2 29	3	3 34	4 85	3 86	317	448	23	
Worle	,,	8 23w	56	10 51	11 31	12 43	17 2	3 33	8 3	4 85	3 5	436	367	488	28	
Milton Road	,,	8 27	10	1	10 56	11 36	12 47		2 37	3 13	3 53	5	85	486	417	528	33	
Weston-s-Mare	arr.	8 30	10	5	11 0	11 40	12 50	1	2 52	4 03	1 73	5 75	1 25	5 26	457	558	37	10*40
(Ashcombe Road)																	

Up Trains. **WEEK DAYS.**

		a.m.	a.m.	a.m.	a.m.	p.m.	p.m.	p.m.	p.m.	p.m.	p.m.	p.m.	p.m.	p.m.	p.m.	p.m.
(Ashcombe Road)																	
Weston-s-Mare	dep.	9	0	10 30	11 10	11 50	1	0 1	0 1	402	503	274	7 5	226	156	553	7 9	5 11* 0
Milton Road	,,	9	3	10 33	11 13	11 53		1 432	533	30	5 256	186	588	109	8	
Worle	,,	9	7	10 37	11 17	11 57	1	71	472	573	334	145	296	227	28	149	12	
Ebdon Lane	,,	9	11	10 41	11 21	12 1		1 503	1 3	36	5 336	267	68	189	16	
Wick St. Lawrence	,,	9	14	10 44	11 24	12 4	41	131	533	4 404	205	376	307	98	229	20	
Ham Lane	,,	9	18	10 48	11 28	12 7		1 563	73	43	5 406	337	128	259	23	
Kingston Road	,,	9	22	10 52	11 32	12 10		1 593	103	53	5 446	377	158	299	27	
Colehouse Lane	,,	9	26	10 56	11 36	12 13		2	23	133	53	5 486	417	188	339	31	
Clevedon	,,	8 w20	9 30	11	0	11 40	12 15	1 28 2	57	3 203	574	375	526	557	203	459	35	11*25
East Clevedon	,,	8 23	9 33		11 43		1 33		3 24		4 41		7 0		3 43		
Walton Park	,,	8 28	9 38	Stop.	11 49	Stop.	1 41	Stop.	3 31	Stop.	4 48	Stop.	7 5	Stop.	3 54	Stop.	
Walton-in-Gordano	,,	8 31	9 41		11 53		1 45		3 34		4 51		7 8		3 58		
Cadbury Road	,,	8 34	9 44		11 58		1 50		3 37		4 54		7 11		9 3		
(Weston-in-Gordano)																	
Clapton Road	,,	8 38	9 48		12 3		1 55		3 41		4 58		7 14		9 8		
Portishead South	,,	8 41	9 51		12 6		1 58		3 44		5 1		7 16		9 11		
Portishead	arr.	8 45	9 55		12 10		2 5		3 52		5 5		7 20		9 15		11*50

NO SUNDAY TRAINS.

W Workmen's Tickets issued on these trains to bonâ fide Workmen only. Saturdays, from Portishead, 9.0 a.m. and 2.17 p.m.; Clevedon to Portishead, 8.20 a.m. and 1.28 p.m.; Clevedon to Weston-super-Mare, 8.5 a.m. and 2.15 p.m.; from Weston-super-Mare and all stations to Clevedon and Portishead, 9.0 a.m. and 2.50 p.m. (Saturdays only)

Passengers must produce their tickets and give them up when required by any of the Company's servants.

Smoking only permitted in the compartments specially allotted for that purpose.

This Table shows the times at which the Trains may be expected to arrive at and depart from the several stations, but their arrival or departure at the times stated is not guaranteed, nor does the Company hold itself responsible for delay or any consequence arising therefrom.

Nat. Tel., Clevedon, 21 x 4   Traffic Office, Clevedon, Sept. 1, 1907.   **G. S. NEWTON, Traffic Manager.**

PRINTED BY THE CLEVEDON PRINTING COMPANY LIMITED, CLEVEDON.

A timetable for September 1907 showing the rarely photographed 2–4–0T locomotive *Portishead* built by Sharp Stewart.

these picked up stone wagons from Black Rock and Conygar quarries, thus saving the expense of a separate goods train. For the last few years of the line's working, the pattern of service was:

	July–Sept.	Apr.–June	Oct.–Mar.
Clevedon–Weston	8	7	7
Clevedon–Portishead	7	6	4

On summer Sundays 5 trains ran to Weston and 3 to Portishead.

In the timetable for 3rd July, 1938 (a typical pre-war year) there were 6 through down trains except on Wednesdays, Thursdays and Saturdays (early closing at Clevedon on Wednesday, and on Thursday at Portishead and Weston) when there were 8. On Wednesdays, Thursdays and Saturdays 3 trains ran from Weston to Clevedon in addition to through ones. There were 6 through up trains (9 on Wednesdays, Thursdays and Saturdays) plus 1 early morning train from Clevedon to Portishead and 1 from Weston to Clevedon. Two extra trains ran from Weston to Clevedon and Clevedon–Portishead every weekday except Thursday. On Wednesdays, Thursdays and Saturdays a late train ran from Weston to Clevedon. Services were quite good on Sundays, the WCPLR running the only train service to Clevedon, as on this day the GWR closed its branch. Three through down trains were run and two from Clevedon to Weston. In the up direction there were three through trains in addition to two from Weston–Clevedon and one from Clevedon–Portishead. Trains were scheduled to take from 60–72 minutes between Portishead and Weston, though two Sunday trains were allowed 55 minutes.

On 11th September, 1939 the service was reduced to three through down trains and two from Clevedon to Weston and the same in the reverse direction. One each way ran between Clevedon and Weston on Sundays. On and after Friday, 1st December, 1939, the 3.55 pm from Clevedon–Weston and the 4.30 pm Weston–Clevedon were cancelled and the Sunday service completely withdrawn.

The line had an unusually large number of stations, there being one on average every ¾ mile, resulting in the possibility of a train stopping every 2–3 minutes.

Before road transport developed and siphoned off some of the passengers, heavy Sunday School specials often had to be divided between Clevedon All Saints' and Walton Park halt, owing to the curves and gradients limiting the engine's hauling capacity. Sunday School trains 7 coaches long have been noted, while guard E. C. Carey recorded a load of 572 tons in the summer of 1926, locomotive *Portishead* hauling twenty-seven 12-ton wagons loaded with stone totalling 513 tons; 2 empty private owners' wagons totalling 14 tons and 3 ex-LSW coaches; this load was not exceptional, about that time five other similar examples being recorded. The longest train known to Carey was thirty-seven empties and two 4-wheeled coaches.[2]

At all but two of the gated level crossings, the fireman ran ahead to open the gates, the conductor being responsible for closing them, though sometimes bystanders would oblige. In the early days, the guard was officially not allowed to leave the train.

In the early days, when a passenger wanted to get out at one of the halts, the guard stood on one side of the train and the conductor on the other, waving a red flag during the day, or swinging a red lamp at night; a green flag or lamp was displayed if there were no passengers wishing to alight. A white light was shown when the train was ready to start.

At night a locomotive crew could not always see passengers waiting at roadside halts, so the more opulent persons flashed a torch, whilst others set fire to their newspaper. Guard Carey fixed a carbide headlamp (from a Sunbeam motor cycle) to the locomotive in addition to the oil lamp, which of course was only of use as a warning. Both railcars carried an electric headlamp which was ideal for spotting potential passengers but tail lamps were not carried.

A passenger recalled:

> One dark night, at Walton-in-Gordano, I heard the train whistling in the distance. If I wanted to catch it, I was told in a rich Somerset accent, I would have to run down the lane to the station. When I got there I would have to 'make a light and wave it about, and then he'll stop for 'ee'. As I ran, I felt in one pocket for an old envelope and in the other for a box of matches. This proved unnecessary since the train was over an hour late and, instead of coming towards Clevedon was on its way to Portishead. I walked home and beat the train by five minutes.

Notes:

1. *Clevedon Mercury*, 7th September, 1907
2. E. C. Carey

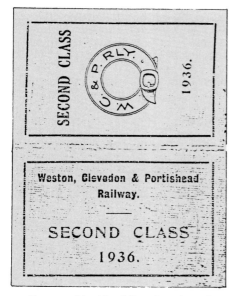

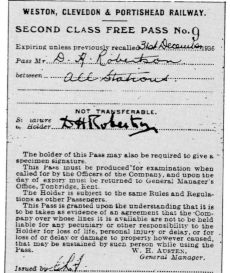

Cover and inside of Free Pass issued to D.H. Robertson, Chapel Hill, Clevedon, who held the contract for maintaining all the company's telephones and electrical equipment.

Chapter Fifteen

Tickets and Fares

E. R. Wintour, traffic manager, designed tickets so that one ticket was available from a certain stopping place to any other station on the line. In 1900 a Worle passenger could pay sixpence and take the whole ticket. For a passenger going to Ham Lane, the conductor would cut off half below 'Ham Lane' so that the passenger's fare of threepence and the clipped off part of the ticket retained by the conductor would account for the sixpence value of the whole ticket. It was a simpler system for working on the cars than stocking tickets from every station to every station.

Trains were known as 'A' and 'B' and these letters were printed on the tickets to facilitate checking the returns. Scissors and punches were kept in cases labelled 'A' or 'B' which measured about 15 in. by 30 in. It is believed that the early tickets were produced by the Clevedon Printing Company. The guard was responsible for collecting tickets.

This system was too clumsy to cope with the extension to Portishead and so tickets of vertical pattern printed by Williamson on soft card were adopted, single tickets being white, the letter 'A' or 'B' still showing according to train. Some twelve months later following a fares' revision, horizontal single tickets were used, the geographical tickets being printed for down journeys in the left hand column and up in the right, the appropriate column being punched to accord with the direction of travel. Later examples of this type of ticket omitted the car letter.

Weekend return tickets issued on Fridays and Saturdays at the cost of a single fare and a third, were available for return by any train up to the following Tuesday. For this concession, a minimum fare of a shilling was stipulated. Day excursion tickets were also available. These were buff with a red 'D' overprinted on both halves, with the addition of a large blue 'X' on the return half. No date appeared on the soft card tickets; ticket numbers providing the only check.

Privilege Return tickets were issued at approximately a quarter of the ordinary return fare. Being buff in colour, these carred a red 'P' overprint on both halves and a large black 'X' on the return portion. Cycle tickets were white and dog tickets green.

During the summer the GWR issued circular tour tickets from Bristol and other stations, passengers travelling by GWR to Weston or Clevedon, (or Portishead after the extension was opened), then travelling over the WCPLR and proceeding by GWR again to their original starting point.

By the time Stephens took over the reins, the most popular of tickets required reprinting, these being replaced by Edmondson card, though the Williamson soft card types continued to be issued for the least common journeys until the line's closure. Edmondson tickets did not carry the car letter, but miniature repeats of the destination appeared at the foot of single tickets. Second class tickets were on light green or purple card.

Edmondson excursion and cheap tickets were buff with a blue 'X' overprinted on the return left hand half. Other overprints were in red: 'D' for day return; 'HDR' half day return; 'T&S' Thursday and Saturday afternoon excursions. 'W', workmen and 'P', privilege. Uncommon journeys, mostly

WESTON, CLEVEDON & PORTISHEAD RAILWAY,

TIME TABLE.

MONDAY, JULY 3rd, 1933

AND UNTIL FURTHER NOTICE.

DOWN TRAINS.   WEEK DAYS.   Sundays

		A M	A M	A M	A M	P M	P M	P M	P M	P M	P M	P M		A M
Portishead	dep.		9 0	10 30	11 55	1 30	3 10	4 35	5 45	7 8	9 20			
Portishead South	,,		9 3	10 33	11 58	1 33	3 13	4 38	5 48	7 11	9 23			
Clapton Road	,,		B	B	B	B	B	B	B	B	B	Wednesdays, and Thursdays, and Saturdays only.		
Cadbury Road	,,		9 7	10 37	12 2	1 37	3 17	4 42	5 52	7 15	9 27			
Walton-in-Gordano	,,		9 11	10 41	12 6	1 41	3 21	4 46	5 56	7 19	9 31			
Walton Park	,,		B	B	B	B	B	B	B	B	B			
Clevedon (All Saints')	,,		9 15	10 45	12 10	1 45	3 25	4 49	6 0	7 23	9 35			
Clevedon East	,,		9 16	10 48	12 11	1 46	3 26	4 51	6 3	7 24	9 36			
Clevedon	,,	8 10	9 35	11 0	12 20	2 15	3 55	5 15	6 10	7 40	9 39		9 45	8 35
Colehouse Lane	,,	B	B	B	B	B	Not Tuesdays	B	Stops	B	Stops		B	B
Kingston Road	,,	8 16	9 41	11 6	12 26	2 21	4 0	5 21		7 46			9 51	8 41
Broadstone	,,	B	B	B	B	B	B	B		B			B	B
Ham Lane	,,	8 19	9 45	11 9	12 29	2 24	4 3	5 24		7 50			9 54	B
Wick St. Lawrence	,,	8 23	9 49	11 13	12 33	2 28	4 7	5 28	Not Tuesdays	7 54			9 58	8 49
Ebdon Lane	,,	B	B	B	B	B	B	B		B			B	B
Worle Town	,,	8 31	9 57	11 21	12 41	2 36	4 14	5 36		8 2			10 6	8 56
Bristol Road	,,	8 34	10 0	11 24	12 44	2 39	4 17	5 39		8 5			10 9	8 59
Milton Road	,,	B	B	B	B	B	B	B		B			B	B
Weston-super-Mare	arr.	8 50	10 6	11 30	12 50	2 45	4 22	5 45		8 11			10 15	9 5

UP TRAINS.   WEEK DAYS.   Sundays

		A M	A M	A M	A M	P M	P M	P M	P M	P M	P M	P M	A M
Weston-super-Mare	dep.		9 0	10 30	11 45	12 58	1 45	3 0	4 30	6 0	8 20	10 30	9 15
Milton Road	,,		B	B	B	B	B	B	B	B	B	B	B
Bristol Road	,,		9 6	10 36	11 50	1 3	1 51	3 6	4 33	6 9	8 26	10 36	9 21
Worle Town	,,		9 9	10 39	11 53	1 7	1 54	3 9	4 36	6 17	8 29	10 39	9 24
Ebdon Lane	,,		B	B	B	B	B	B	B	B	B	B	B
Wick St. Lawrence	,,		9 17	10 47	12 0	1 15	2 2	3 17	4 44	6 21	8 37	10 43	9 31
Ham Lane	,,		9 21	10 51	12 4	1 19	2 5	3 20	4 48	6 24	8 41	10 47	B
Broadstone	,,		B	B	B	b	B	B	B	B	B	B	B
Kingston Road	,,		9 24	10 54	12 9	1 22	2 8	3 24	4 51	6 27	8 45	10 51	9 38
Colehouse Lane	,,		B	B	B	B	B	B	B	B	B	B	B
Clevedon	,,	7 0	9 35	11 5	12 20	1 28	2 14	3 35	5 5	6 33	8 50	10 56	9 45
Clevedon East	,,	7 20	9 38	11 8	12 23	Stops.	2 46	3 38	5 8	6 36	8 53	Stops.	Stops.
Clevedon (All Saints')	,,	7 22	9 39	11 9	12 24		2 47	3 39	5 10	6 37	8 55		
Walton Park	,,	7 25	B	B	B		B	B	B	B	B		
Walton-in-Gordano	,,	7 28	9 43	11 13	12 28		2 51	3 43	5 14	6 41	8 59		
Cadbury Road	,,	7 32	9 47	11 17	12 32		2 55	3 47	5 18	6 45	9 3		
Clapton Road	,,	B	B	B	B		B	B	B	B	B		
Portishead South	,,	7 35	9 51	11 22	12 36		2 59	3 51	5 26	6 48	9 7		
Portishead	arr.	7 45	10 0	11 30	12 45		3 2	4 5	5 30	6 56	9 15		

The Company reserve the right to Withdraw any of the above Trains without previous Notice.
B Stops by Signal to pick up or set down passengers as required
Special arrangements for quick and Cheap Delivery of Parcels and Goods.   Special Service on Bank Holidays.
Workmen's Tickets at Reduced Fares are issued daily only to bona fide Workmen and available only to return by any train after 2 p.m. each day, and are available only on day of issue.

SPECIAL TRIPS ARRANGED FOR PARTIES AT REDUCED FARES.

CHEAP RETURN TICKETS will be issued Daily as under:—

	2nd Class Return Fares. s. d.
WESTON-SUPER-MARE to WORLE All Trains	0 3
WESTON-SUPER-MARE and MILTON ROAD to CLEVEDON & CLEVEDON EAST. At 10.30 a.m., 11.45 a.m., 12.58 p.m., 3.0 p.m. *4.30 p.m. and 6.0 p.m. *Not Tuesdays	1 0
WESTON-SUPER-MARE and MILTON ROAD to PORTISHEAD and PORTISHEAD SOUTH. At 10.30 a.m., 11.45 a.m., 3.0 p.m. and *4.30 p.m. *Not Tuesdays	1 9
WORLE to WESTON-SUPER-MARE. All Trains	0 3
WORLE to CLEVEDON. At 11.53 a.m. 3.9 p.m. and *4.36 p.m. *Not Tuesdays.	0 9
WORLE to PORTISHEAD and PORTISHEAD SOUTH. At 11.53 a.m. and 3.9 p.m.	1 6
WICK ST. LAWRENCE to WESTON-SUPER-MARE. At 9.49 a.m., 12.33 a.m., 2.28 p.m. and 5.28 p.m.	0 6
CLAPTON ROAD to WESTON-SUPER-MARE. At 9.3 a.m., 12.2 p.m. and 1.37 p.m.	1 8
WALTON-IN-GORDANO to WESTON-SUPER-MARE. At 9.11 a.m., 12.6 p.m. and 1.41 p.m.	1 3

	2nd Class Return Fares. s. d.
WALTON PARK to WESTON-SUPER-MARE. At 9.11 a.m., 12.6 p.m. and 1.41 p.m.	1 3
CLEVEDON EAST to WESTON-SUPER-MARE. At 9.16 a.m. 10.48 a.m., 12.11 p.m., 1.46 p.m. and 4.51 p.m.	1 0
CLEVEDON to WESTON-SUPER-MARE. All Trains At 9.35 a.m., 11.0 a.m., 12.20 p.m., 2.15 p.m. *3.55 p.m. and 5.15 p.m. *Not Tuesdays.	1 0
CLEVEDON to WORLE. At 11.0 a.m. and 2.15 p.m.	0 9
CLEVEDON EAST to PORTISHEAD and PORTISHEAD. At 11.8 a.m., *2.46 p.m. and 3.38 p.m. *Not Tuesdays	0 9
CLEVEDON to PORTISHEAD and PORTISHEAD SOUTH. At 11.5 a.m., *2.43 p.m., 3.35 p.m., *5.5 p.m. and 6.33 p.m. *Not Tuesdays	0 9
WALTON-IN-GORDANO to PORTISHEAD SOUTH and PORTISHEAD. All Trains	0 6
WALTON-IN-GORDANO to CLEVEDON EAST and CLEVEDON All Trains	0 6
CADBURY ROAD to CLEVEDON EAST & CLEVEDON. All Trains	0 7
CADBURY ROAD to PORTISHEAD SOUTH and PORTISHEAD. All Trains	0 6

	2nd Class Return Fares. s. d.
PORTISHEAD and PORTISHEAD SOUTH to WESTON-SUPER-MARE. At 9.0 a.m., 10.30 a.m., and 1.30 p.m.	1 9
PORTISHEAD and PORTISHEAD SOUTH to WORLE. At 9.0 a.m. and 1.30 p.m.	1 6
PORTISHEAD and PORTISHEAD SOUTH to CLEVEDON and CLEVEDON EAST. At 9.0 a.m., 1.30 p.m., 4.35 p.m., *5.45 p.m., and 7.8 p.m. *Not Tuesdays	0 9
COLEHOUSE LANE to WESTON-SUPER-MARE. At 9.35 a.m., 11.6 a.m. and 2.21 p.m.	0 9
KINGSTON ROAD to WESTON-SUPER-MARE. At 9.41 a.m., 11.6 a.m. and 2.21 p.m.	0 11
HAM LANE to WESTON-SUPER-MARE. At 9.45 a.m., 12.29 p.m., 2.24 p.m. and 5.24 p.m.	0 8
EBDON LANE to WESTON-SUPER-MARE. At 11.13 a.m. and 2.28 p.m.	0 5
BRISTOL ROAD to WESTON-SUPER-MARE. All Trains	0 3
HAM LANE to CLEVEDON. At 10.51 a.m., 12.4 p.m., 3.20 p.m. and *4.48 p.m. *Not Tuesdays	0 6
WICK ST. LAWRENCE At 10.47 a.m., 12 noon, 3.17 p.m. and *4.44 p.m. *Not Tuesday	0 6

Passengers Holding Cheap Day Tickets are allowed to alight at any Station short of destination in either direction on surrender of Ticket, and to return from any intermediate Station.

AVAILABLE TO RETURN BY ANY TRAIN ON DAY OF ISSUE ONLY.

See Handbills re Special Cheap Excursion Tickets, at Attractive Fares, Wednesday, Thursday, and Saturday Afternoons.
Week End Tickets at about a Single Fare and one Third for the Return Journey are now issued on Fridays and Saturdays between any two Stations and are available to return by any Train up to the following Tuesday.   Minimum Fare 1/-

All Cheap Tickets issued to and from Weston-super-Mare are available at Milton Road Station. For particulars apply any Station or Traffic Office, Clevedon.
Children under Three Years of age, Free ; Three and under Fourteen, Half-price.
The Tickets are not transferable. Should a Cheap Ticket be used by any other train than specified above, it will be rendered void, and thereupon the fare paid will be liable to forfeiture and the full ordinary fare will become chargeable.
Information respecting Rates for Goods and Parcels Traffic and other arrangements can be made on application to

Traffic Office, Clevedon, June, 1933.   C.10,680.   Telephone 69 Clevedon.   **W. H. AUSTEN,** Manager.

CLEVEDON PRINTING CO. LIMITED

first class, were written on pink blank cards.[1] On occasions when ticket supplies for a particular journey were exhausted, a ticket of similar value would be issued with the destination altered in ink. Stephens himself had a polished aluminium free pass with a hole punched for it to be hung on his watch chain. It was oval in shape and bore the lettering 'Weston, Clevedon & Portishead Rly. No. 1'.

Prior to closure, a cheap day return from Weston to Portishead cost 1s. 10d. except on Thursday and Saturday afternoons when it was reduced to 1s. 4d. The Weston to Clevedon cheap fare was 1s. 1d. and 9½d. on Thursdays and Saturdays. Cheap tickets were issued daily from all intermediate stations to Weston by nearly all trains at single fare for the double journey, and from several stations to Clevedon and Portishead.

A company regulation stated that,

> at all intermediate stations fares will be received and tickets issued, conditionally only on there being room in the train. In case there should not be sufficient room for all the passengers to or for whom any such tickets shall have been issued, the holders of such as shall be the longest distance, shall, as far as is reasonably practicable, have the preference, and the holders of such as shall be for the same distance shall, as far as is reasonably practicable, have priority according to the orders in which such tickets shall have been issued, as denoted by the numbers stamped thereon.

An unfortunate incident occurred in 1902 through a passenger not understanding conditions under which tickets were issued. He paid a shilling for a return ticket from Weston-super-Mare to Clevedon and wished to break his journey back at Wick St Lawrence. The conductor informed him that this was inadmissible and the return half of the ticket would have to be surrendered if he got off. The passenger ducked under the conductor's arms, damaging his own hat in the process. Later he had to pay 4d. excess fare Wick to Weston.

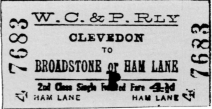

Running Sunday trains meant that a guard would work a seven day week, alternate weeks. Sunday trains were nearly always worked by railcars, the large one to Weston-super-Mare in the morning collecting full churns outwards and dropping off empties on its return, the small railcar being used for the trip to Portishead. The guard's turns were:

Winter
Early turn: 7.30 am–12.30 pm; 2.0 pm–5.30 pm
Late turn: 10.0 am–2.0 pm; 3.45 pm–8.35 pm
Summer
Early turn: 7.0 am–12.30 pm; 2.0 pm–5.30 pm
Late turn: 8.0 am–2.0 pm; 3.45 pm–9.30 pm Mon, Tues, Fri; 11.0 pm Wed, Thurs, Sat.
Sunday turn:8.0 am–10.0 am; 4.15 pm–6.15 pm

On 1st January, 1908 the company's parcel service began, parcels being collected and delivered within a mile of Weston, Clevedon and Portishead stations for the inclusive rates of:

Not exceeding:
    3 lb.   4d.
    7 lb.   5d.
    28 lb. 6d.

This innovation proved popular as it did on contemporary suburban electric tramways. An interesting extension of this service was that during the last two weeks of July 1908, all passengers who purchased goods over a value of ten shillings at the summer sale of the Weston-super-Mare draper's, Messrs Lance & Lance, had their return fare on the WCPLR refunded by the store, in addition to the free express delivery of their goods; this arrangement continued annually until 1922.

Notes:

1. Much of the information in this chapter came from the *Railway Magazine* 1973, p. 71, article by K. Montague

Locomotive *Portishead* at Walton Park with a 6-coach train, 1938. Wagons in the siding are for Conygar Quarry.   *B.J. Miller Collection*

Chapter Sixteen

Accidents

One of the earliest mishaps on the Railway occurred on 5th June, 1899 when the locomotive and two cars forming the 11 am from Weston to Clevedon and loaded with about 30 passengers, was derailed approaching Kingston Seymour. It ploughed along the permanent way before being brought to a standstill. Fortunately none of the passengers was hurt, and not long elapsed before a locomotive and car were dispatched from Clevedon to pick them up. A breakdown gang set to work and by 7 pm had the two cars back on the road and the line was finally cleared late that same evening. Except for the breaking of a 'coupling bar' (chain?) the locomotive and cars received no damage. The accident was said to have been caused by the heat of the sun expanding the rails.

On 31st August, 1903 the 1.15 pm Clevedon to Weston-super-Mare hauled by the Sharp Stewart 2−4−0T *Portishead* was approaching Worle level crossing which was worked by the 71 year-old-Joseph Sperring. When the train was 100 yds from the crossing, he waved a flag and shouted at an approaching wagonette, but the driver ignored him. In the ensuing collision two died and four were seriously injured by the train. Newton wrote[1] in 1940:

> I well remember the Bristol Road (Worle) accident, I was sat on the steps of the last coach. I was reading the *Daily Telegraph*. I'll never forget it as long as I live. I did not eat any solid food for weeks after what I saw.

Although the railway was not at fault, the Board of Trade observed that the train was not fitted with continuous brakes; the gates did not close across the road and failed to project sufficiently far into the road when closed to road traffic and to leave no doubt in the minds of road users that the road was obstructed.

Soon after the opening of the extension to Portishead a mishap occurred on this section. On Saturday 10th August, 1907 as the last train was returning from Portishead to Clevedon, the locomotive collided with two horses which had strayed on the line. One animal was killed and the other injured. The train kept to the rails, but was subject to a considerable delay.

A similar incident happened 12 months later on 30th August, 1908 when the last train from Weston to Clevedon killed two heifers near Colehouse Lane, the second coach being derailed and damaged.

Ungated level crossings were highly dangerous at night to those unfamiliar with the locality as the unlit warning signs could not be seen. In 1909 Ernest Price from Sheffield sent the following letter to the Board of Trade following an unfortunate experience at Walton Park.[2]

SIR,

Re Light Railway, Portishead to Clevedon

> Last week I made a journey by night between the two towns named above, and I found at one part of the road a condition of things so dangerous that I think it important to call your attention thereto. The Light Railway crosses the main road, at what I think is an angle of about 30 degrees, and there are no gates to protect the road and no signs of any sort to warn the cyclist.

The 1.15 p.m. express train (engine and 2 bogie carriages) Clevedon to Weston, ran into a one-horse wagonette at the level crossing near Worle. The horse was pushed into a ditch and the wagonette across the hedge. The driver was thrown out and injured. The six occupants of the wagonette were all thrown out under the wheels of the leading carriage; 2 were killed and 4 severely injured. The horse was not much injured, and the damage to the wagonette was not nearly as great as would have been expected.

The carriages were fitted for the vacuum brake, but the engine was not; there was a separate conductor on each carriage to attend to the hand brake.

Worle level crossing is about 2 miles from Weston-super-Mare, which is one terminus of the Weston, Clevedon and Portishead light railway. The railway crosses the road from Weston to Worle at an angle of 45°. The line is practically level on both sides of the crossing, and is straight for a considerable distance on each side of it, so that the driver of a train approaching the crossing obtains a good view of it. On each side of the road there are gates about 10 ft. wide which close across the light railway completely, but when they are opened for a train to run through them they do not close across the road at all, and they are indeed not visible from the road until quite close to them. The gates are provided with targets, and a gatekeeper is stationed at the crossing to open the gates when necessary, and to stop the traffic along the road. There is a low edge on the side of the road, but this does not in any way prevent the driver of a vehicle in the road obtaining a clear view of the light railway. The roadway is about 20 feet in width and is quite level; the approach to the crossing is straight for about 200 yards in the Worle direction, so that the driver of a vehicle approaching from that village obtains a good view of the crossing.

There is a small platform alongside the light railway situated about 20 yards from the crossing and on the Worle side of it. Trains frequently stop at this platform to pick up and put down passengers, but the train on this occasion was one which was not timed to stop there.

At points on the railway about 300 yds. on each side of the level crossing there are notice boards warning drivers to reduce their speed to 8 miles an hour, and at points on the road about 50 yds. on each side of the crossing there are also notice boards warning drivers to beware of the trains.

Smart, the driver of the wagonette, saw the train approaching; he noticed it was slackening speed, and concluded that it was going to stop at the platform before reaching the crossing. He intended to cross in front of the engine. When close to the crossing he saw that the train was not stopping, and at the same moment his horse took fright. He tried to pull the horse into the hedge on the right of the road, but was unable to do so, and apparently the point of the left shaft came into collision with the side of the engine. Smart states positively that there was no signalman in the road waving a red flag, and that he did not hear anyone shouting to him.

Flagman Sperring, who was on duty at the crossing at the time, states positively that he saw the wagonette about 100 yards from the crossing, and at once commenced to wave his red flag, standing in the road near the gate post on the Worle side. As the driver of the wagonette took no notice of the red flag, Sperring shouted to him at the top of his voice, but the driver still paid no attention, and appeared to be urging his horse to go faster, with the result that the wagonette ran into the engine when the latter was on the level crossing. The driver of the engine – Jones – observed the flagman, as did also two civilians.

The responsibility for this accident rests on Smart, who appears to have acted very recklessly, and no blame attaches to any of the railway servants. All witnesses, including Smart, agree that the train was going at a moderate speed.

The train was not provided, as it should have been, with a continuous brake.

The Company has fully carried out the obligations placed on it by Parliament. It is, however, admitted that the vehicular traffic along the main road is considerable in summer time, and in the face of this accident some further precaution seems desirable.

The gates, as at present hung, are not visible from the road until quite close to them, but there would be no difficulty in hanging them so that when opened they would each project for their length of 10 ft. into the road; there could then be no possible excuse for the driver of a vehicle pleading that he did not know that he was prohibited from using the crossing. The Company should therefore consider the advisability of carrying out this alteration at the two level crossings of the Bristol road, near Worle.

An official report of the accident near Worle on the 31st August, 1903, as reported in the *Railway Engineer* of 1904.

I myself was cycling with two boys on a moonless night. We saw the train when it was in an adjacent field, and heard its whistles, but we had no idea it was going to cross the high road. The more I recall it, the more do I marvel at the wonder of our escape. We were within a few yards of the crossing (as it proved to be) when the train suddenly crossed the road at a fair speed right in front of us.

We sprang from our machines as quickly as we could, and looked at each other in horror as we realised what an awful thing it would have been if one or other had been a few yards on, or had not had sufficient presence of mind to apply the brake and jump off.

I feel that some tragedy will be acted at this spot if something is not done for the protection of travellers, and sincerely trust that this report of our experience will help to prevent any such sad occurrence.

I am, Sir,
Yours sincerely,
Ernest Price

To prevent an accident, the company agreed to stop trains before crossing the cattle grid.

A very minor mishap occurred c.1912 on a mixed train at Clevedon. An old dumb buffer low-sided wagon was being shunted and during these operations, a buffer which had rotted, collapsed, derailing the truck. In getting the wagon back on the road, the locomotive *Clevedon* became derailed. The train finally left 1½ hours late.

On 12th December, 1925 the 6.33 pm Clevedon to Portishead killed two steers and a heifer at Weston-in-Gordano. When the case for compensation came before Yatton County Court, the proceedings made interesting reading[3] and show how the company was esteemed. Wilshire, for the plaintiff, said to part time driver Albert Sharpe, 'I take it you are a part time driver, and chaser of cattle off the line?' His Honour, 'I should think that a journey from Clevedon to Portishead must be fraught with much interest, but, if in a hurry, I think I should prefer to walk.' Further examined, driver Sharpe said that after the accident he took the train on the Cadbury Road and then backed it towards the scene of the accident. Mr Wilshire, 'Rather an habitual form of progress on that line – a little bit forward and a little bit backward.' Colonel Stephens revealed that between 1918 and 1926 the company had put in 8700 posts and 20 miles of fencing, using 20¼ miles of wire since 1922.

The evening of 29th December, 1926 had the makings of a disaster. As locomotive *Clevedon* was crossing Wick Bridge towards Weston-super-Mare a coupling rod broke, dug into a sleeper causing all the wheels on one side to be lifted. Thankfully it sank down, on and not off the track. The loose rod then punctured a water tank. Sixteen-year-old conductor Arthur Jenkins walked to Wick St Lawrence to phone for assistance, but found the telephone out of order. Fortunately the instrument on the Wharf was not too far away, though he was unable to call the attention of anyone at Clevedon. He phoned Gordon Grundy, the Weston-super-Mare station master who alerted his brother at Clevedon by means of the external (GPO) line. No spare locomotive or crew was available, but driver Sharpe and fireman Plumley were told that by the time they had walked back to Clevedon a locomotive would be available. *Clevedon* was pushed into the loop to be towed back

The Clevedon Mercury's photograph of the collapse of a small bridge, whilst *Hesperus* was shunting wagons onto the jetty on 5th April, 1934.

Courtesy Clevedon Mercury

LEVEL-CROSSING SMASH, on the 19th March, 1932. Wrecked motor-coach and (above) derailed petrol rail car after a collision at Bristol Road level crossing. The motor-coach was carrying a party of Rugby footballers. Six people, including two passengers in the train, were hurt.

next morning. The conductor's father, alarmed at the non-appearance of his son well past the usual time, went to the station to make enquiries, but found no one other than the night fitter who was quite oblivious of the fact that one of his engines was missing.

In 1936 guard Carey was looking out approaching Walton Park Halt to see if there were any passengers and noticed a rear driving wheel wobbling on *Portishead*. He immediately applied the vacuum brake as the rear axle had broken. A telephone was used to call for assistance and No. 5 came to the rescue with fitter Hill. *Portishead's* fire was put out, the engine jacked up in Walton Park loop and the wheels sent to the Shropshire & Montgomeryshire Railway shops for a new axle to be fitted. The locomotive rested on sleepers at Walton Park for about a month.

A rather similar mishap occurred some three years earlier when No. 3 *Weston* was backing into Black Rock with the 1.35 pm from Portishead to drop off empty stone wagons, the centre axle breaking. A relief engine arrived within an hour, fitter Hill driving, the shed man firing. No spare engine was kept in steam, the first available locomotive had its fire lit, and as soon as 80 lb. of steam was available, they set off, struggling to raise full pressure on the way. The rods and springs were removed, the centre wheels jacked up by 1½ in. and secured by a wire hawser round the footplate, *Weston* becoming a temporary 0−4−0T. The relief engine was coupled in front of *Weston* and worked the train to Clevedon arriving about 3.30 pm, in time to clear the section for the 3.35 pm Clevedon to Portishead.[4]

Accidents continued to occur at ungated level crossings, and at Worle in particular. One such incident happened in October 1937 when a lorry struck a railcar. A passenger was seriously injured, dying a month later. Traffic lights did not completely cure the problem, as on 7th September, 1938 the 2.00 pm Clevedon to Weston consisting of four coaches and a locomotive running bunker first (presumably No. 4) was struck by a motor cyclist on the crossing. He was turning his head talking to his pillion passenger and failed to notice the train or lights; regrettably he and his passenger were killed.

On 19th March, 1932 the small Drewry railcar was struck on the Bristol Road crossing by a Bristol Tramways & Carriage Company's coach carrying a party of rugby footballers; four people in the coach and two in the railcar were hurt. On 27th August, 1937 the small railcar was derailed after it had been in collision with a lorry on the Baytree Road level crossing at Weston-super-Mare.

Notes:

1. PRO: ZSPC 11/388
2. PRO: MT6.2484/5
3. *Clevedon Mercury*, 26th June, 1926
4. E. C. Carey

Three views of a derailment near Kingston Road in 1898. The locomotive *Weston* and one of the American coaches were involved. The bottom view shows locomotive *Portishead* in attendance. Note the flimsy fencing.　　　*(All) G. Rushton Collection*

Chapter Seventeen

Tales and Personalities

All light railways have amusing stories connected with them and the WCPLR was no exception. In the summer of 1908, a Welsh newspaper[1] printed the following:

> Among other novelties that delight visitors to Weston-super-Mare and Clevedon these holiday times, are the wonderful ways of the Weston, Clevedon and Portishead Railway, whereon time is no object, and running schedules are regarded as vain things. One day last week, the so-called 3.45 train left Clevedon for Weston, and skimmed along for four or five miles, ignoring the claims of intermediate stations for something like a quarter of an hour. Then it transpired that an angry clergyman, who was travelling with his worthy help meet, had booked for the intermediate station which had been left a few miles in the rear. The error of the train in skipping that important station had, therefore, grievously disappointed and discommoded him. The railway officials, however, were quite equal to the occasion. To the amazement of all and sundry they simply ordered the train to push back again over the single line to the station some miles behind near Clevedon, and this in a manner soothed the reverend gentlemen.

Some of the rules and regulations brought a smile to the face, one particularly interesting one read:

> Except by the express permission of the guard of the train, a person of the male sex above or apparently above the age of eight years, shall not travel, or attempt to travel or remain in any compartment of a carriage marked or notified as being reserved or appropriated for the exclusive use of persons of the female sex.

In the autumn it was not unknown for the driver and fireman of the first train from Clevedon to Weston to warn the guard with three short whistles and stop *en route* to pick mushrooms. These were fried with bacon on a shovel on arrival at Weston. At least one person was able to fulfil his ambition to pick blackberries from a moving train on the WCPLR, while Ebdon Lane waiting room had scratched on the wall 'Passengers are requested not to pick blackberries while the train is in motion'. At some level crossings children got out when the train stopped, to pick flowers and then refused to get back. One small boy threw his mother's handbag out of the carriage window and the train dutifully stopped so that it could be retrieved. Gordon Grundy, station master at Weston-super-Mare, rather foolishly left the key in the lock of his office door, tempting a schoolgirl to turn it and lock him in.

All underbridges were without decking, catwalks being provided for the staff. One passenger helping to push the broken-down small Drewry railcar back to Clevedon one night, stepped between the sleepers of an underline bridge and fell into the green slime below.[2] 1908 saw an interesting story in the *Clevedon Mercury*[3] headed:

Fracas on the Light Railway

> A scene of no little excitement was witnessed at the Bristol Road crossing of the Weston and Clevedon Light Railway Co., on Whit-Tuesday evening. Whilst a down train was approaching, a party of some half-dozen cyclists rode up with the apparent intention of crossing in front of the train. The crossing keeper, Hood,

knowing that the train was to run through the crossing without stopping, at once raised his red flag and shouted to the party to dismount. His warnings, however, produced not the slightest effect on one of the cyclists who quickened his speed, bent on the foolhardy feat of crossing in front of the approaching engine. There was no time to be lost in mincing matters, and, realising the gravity of the situation, Hood promptly took the initiative, as well as administered a salutary lesson to the reckless cyclist, by pushing him, machine and all, into the abutting hedge. Seeing that within a few seconds the train was on the crossing one would have thought that the rider, on disengaging himself and the cycle from the hedge, would have realised that he had received nothing more than he deserved. So far from this being case, however, he commenced to roughly use the crossing-keeper, in which matter he was supported by his colleagues. Mr. G. S. Newton, the Manager of the line, happened to be on the train and, on the engine being brought to a standstill, at once proceeded to quell the disturbance, as well as to caution, the cyclists as to their future behaviour. The train was thereupon re-started, but before it had proceeded many yards the cyclists — apparently considering there was no possibility of further interruption — again commenced their attack on the unoffending crossing-keeper. The matter, however, did not escape the observation of those on the train, with the result that the engine was reversed and run back to the scene of the disturbance. This time the names and addresses of the militant wheelers were taken, and it is probable that a sequel will be forthcoming to their unwarrantable action.

PERSONALITIES

W. H. Austen, Colonel Stephens' engineering assistant from 1892, was appointed traffic manager in 1931 on Stephens' death and saw the final decline and demise of the line. A tall, upright, imposing figure, he won the respect of his staff. He never gave a warning of a visit, thereby hoping to keep men on the alert. If all was well, a tip would be given, but he would not tolerate slackness.

John Francis Ranald Daniel, born 25th November, 1829 and after studying law and civil engineering, was appointed Secretary and manager of the Bristol Athenaeum, a post he relinquished when he became Secretary to the Bristol & Portishead Pier & Railway Company (incorporated in 1863). He was also appointed Secretary and general manager of the Portishead gas and water companies. He occupied his spare time as an instructor in the First Gloucestershire Volunteer Rifle Corps. In 1885 he was appointed general manager of the Midland & South Western Junction Railway and with his brother A. F. R. Daniel as Secretary, they held the posts until 1892. Daniel was appointed Secretary of the WCPT and Managing Director of the WCPLR. An old man, he faded from the railway in 1911 and died at Mells, near Frome, on 23rd December, 1918.

Spencer Gore-Browne of Oakwood Court, Kensington, was appointed Chairman of the WCPLR in 1907 and, holding the post for 25 years, was cousin of C. E. Heath's wife; Heath being Managing Director of the Excess Insurance Company. Gore-Browne based in London, was chief accountant of the Great Indian Peninsular Railway and Chairman of the Cleobury Mortimer & Dittons Prior Light Railway in Shropshire. Early in 1909 he was appointed Receiver and general manager of the WCPLR. His half-sovereign tips to the train crews made his visits popular; he was not averse to dipping his hand into his pocket to help the company. He died in January 1933, the vacant office being filled by H. E. Fulford, a Lincoln's Inn barrister, who accepted no remuneration.

Arthur J. Grundy, formerly on the staff of the Kent & East Sussex Railway, was appointed by Stephens as manager at the Clevedon headquarters, retaining this position until 1935. His two brothers were also employed on the line. Gordon, station master at Weston-super-Mare and Sidney, who held a similar position at Clevedon and was a jolly, plump, little Dickensian type of man, later transferred to Portishead, only to be made redundant in 1938 as an economy measure. Arthur himself had been declared redundant in May 1935.

That the line managed to last until 1940 was due largely to the efforts of Cuthbert Eden Heath, founder and Managing Director of the Excess Insurance Company. He lived at Tonbridge where Stephens had his headquarters. Although not a railway enthusiast, he persisted in keeping the line open and even developing it, probably hoping that one day the Great Western would see its way clear to making an attractive offer. He died on 3rd March, 1939 never realising his dream.

H. H. Matthews, Secretary of the WCPLR from 1907 until 1911, was a partner in G. F. Hudson, Matthews & Company of 32, Queen Victoria Street, London EC4, a firm which remained the WCPLR's solicitors until closure. Matthews was the originator of the Weston-super-Mare Junction Light Railway.

George S. Newton was appointed General Manager on the departure of Edward Wintour in 1903. Newton had worked himself up the promotional ladder. First joining the company as a booking clerk at Weston-super-Mare when the office opened there in Easter 1898, two years later saw him appointed accountant at Clevedon. When Wintour resigned as traffic manager and locomotive superintendent in 1903, he nominated young Newton as his successor. Newton left and emigrated to Canada when Gore-Browne was appointed Receiver in August 1911. In a letter of 30th September, 1940 to J. H. P. Capell, a Weston-super-Mare solicitor whose father had owned the land on which the terminus was built, Newton wrote[4] regarding the WCPLR's finances.

> I know my pocket had to suffer and my family very often because there was no funds and the men's wages had to be paid above anyone else; many a week passed by in the winter time when men only used to receive so much on account and balance just when we were able to get it in.

Newton was succeeded by Major (later Lieutenant Colonel) Holman Frederick Stephens, born 31st October, 1868. Finishing his education at University College, London and on the continent, he served an apprenticeship at the locomotive and carriage shops of the Metropolitan Railway at Neasden. Following appointment as Engineer to several railway companies, he went on to become associated with eleven light railways, both standard and narrow gauge. He was appointed General Manager, Engineer and locomotive superintendent of the WCPLR in 1911, his interest in classical Greek and Roman mythology explaining the choice of names for some of his locomotives. He was given the rank of Lieutenant Colonel in the Royal

Engineers for his war service in Britain between 1914 and 1916. Chairman of the Association of Railways of Local Interest (later the Association of Minor Railways), he held official responsibility in 11 of its 23 members. Stephens, a large man with brown leggings and breeches, had a powerful innovative personality, was good at getting his own way and could make do with a minimum of finance. He certainly did his best with the line and sought new traffic, opening halts, introducing concrete sleepers and building a wharf, while the introduction of internal combustion engined vehicles reduced running costs. A gentleman who appreciated loyalty, he sent a letter of thanks to every employee who stayed at his job during the 1926 General Strike. Based at his headquarters at Salford Terrace, Tonbridge, Kent, he only visited the line periodically, giving the staff notice of his inspection; he stayed at the Grand Atlantic Hotel, Weston-super-Mare. Suffering a number of strokes during his last year which caused him to be partially paralysed and unable to speak, he died at Dover on 23rd October, 1931.

Edward R. Wintour was a rolling stone. He started working with the Severn & Wye Railway at Lydney where he spent four years in the manager's office and a further three in the locomotive department. He then had the experience of a year at sea, followed by five years dealing with a different kind of water in the engineering department of Lambeth Waterworks, followed by four years with Bristol Waterworks. About June 1897 the WCPT appointed him traffic manager and locomotive superintendent. While working for the WCPT he lived just by Weston station at 88, Ashcombe Road, which was also the company's offices and is now a chemist's shop. Wintour resigned in 1903 to take up the appointment of Engineer to Lambeth Waterworks. Newton wrote[5] in 1940:

> I still believe Mr Wintour saw the writing on the wall, that is why he took that post in London and when he left the Light Railway the Directors were seeking a new man to take over management and Wintour would not listen to their engaging anyone else but me, he knew I could handle the ropes as well as himself and young as I was at that time, it was 'Newton's job' and I got it without a hitch.

Archie Judd was the man at Tonbridge responsible for making out the company's weekly revenue return and carrying out other paperwork. Between 1911 and 1916 R. E. Hall was Company Secretary, being succeeded by F. E. Johnson, Secretary of the Excess Insurance Company. S. J. W. Nott was the WCPT's accountant, leaving the company's employ in 1902 with five half-yearly accounts not presented. His office was filled by A. J. Willis of Sanderstead whose principal employer was the South Eastern & Chatham Railway. Victor Ware rose from a 17s. 6d. a week office boy at Clevedon to £2. 10s. 0d. a week station agent at Portishead, this latter term covering tasks from the lowliest porter/shunter to the exalted rank of station master. Ware was the nephew of Frank Beere, himself station master at Portishead until moved to Arthur Grundy's desk at Clevedon.

The staff wore a navy blue uniform consisting of:

> two pairs of trousers or breeches with ⅛ in. red piping down the seam;
> one waistcoat with a single row of brass buttons down the front, 3 pockets and an adjustable back strap;

one double-breasted top coat with double row of brass buttons, 2 large side pockets
    and inside pocket, 'WC&PR' stitched on collar in red cotton;
one peaked cap with 1 in. high letters 'WC&PR' in red, black leather chin strap
    secured by two buttons;
one red tie.[6]

Guards wore breeches and black leggings because of the long grass; Riddick
wore them habitually, and Carey only occasionally. The uniforms were
given by the company and supplied by Hiatt's, outfitters, Old Street,
Clevedon.

The two guards, Jack Riddick and E. C. (Dan) Carey had considerable
autonomy, deciding daily what vehicles would be required; whether a coach
should be left at Weston for strengthening later in the day. Riddick had Car
'A' set of tickets and Carey Car 'B'. Riddick, the head guard, received £3 a
week and Carey £1 17s. 6d. On a Bank Holiday each would collect about £25
in fares,[7] this not including cash taken at booking offices at Weston, Clevedon and Portishead. A guard was required to help coal an engine if the crew
were tight on time, which could happen if Conygar Quarry had heavy traffic
and a special trip was required.[8]

Although in the early days the duties of conductor and guard were carried
out by two separate individuals, latterly they were worked by just one
person, the change probably taking place during World War I to ease the
manpower shortage. This extra task made a guard's life hectic: issuing
tickets, closing level crossing gates; dealing with passengers and parcels
traffic; shunting mixed trains.

Notes:
1. Quoted in the *Weston Mercury*, 5th September, 1908
2. Windeatt
3. *Clevedon Mercury*, 16th June, 1908
4. PRO: ZSPC 11/388
5. Letter from George Newton to J. H. P. Capell 30th September, 1940, PRO: ZSPC
   11/388
6. E. C. Carey
7. *Ibid*
8. *Ibid*

W.H. Austen

John Francis
Ronald Daniel

Lt Col Holman
Frederick Stephens

Chapter Eighteen

Epilogue

Ronald Bailey in the *Weston Mercury* of 16th November, 1951 neatly sums up the line:

> (The Light Railway) . . . had the misfortune to be born just a year or two before motors cars had passed the freak stage, and, as a result, it had to struggle against fierce competition almost all its life. Yet to many people it was indispensible. To others, it was a unique pleasure.
>
> To pass between hedgerows powdered with may-blossom, lush green, daisied meadows and golden carpets of buttercups, orchards in carnival dress, fat healthy cows and placidly grazing sheep, to see how the train disturbed wild life, sending rabbits scurrying to their burrows, startling crows from the line and causing lapwings to soar away to other fields; to see these things was to know the real heart of Somerset.

THE SITE TODAY

There are now few traces left of the WCPLR. The station site at Weston-super-Mare can still be located. Piers of the Yeo Bridge and the Wharf are still there, but regrettably cannot be visited as they lie on private land. The trackbed of the line is very difficult to trace between Weston and Clevedon due to lack of earthworks, but is a little more visible in the Gordano Valley where it ran on a low embankment. The concrete banks at both Conygar and Black Rock quarry sidings where narrow gauge wagons tipped stone into standard gauge wagons are still extant, though that at the latter location has had earth banked up against it. These two locations are visible from the public road. At Portishead the WCPLR bridge across a rhine can be seen from Wyndham Way, while the archway which led to Portishead station can still be seen to the left of the White Lion Inn, High Street.

Nailsea Model Railway Club have built a 7 mm. to the foot model of the WCPLR and when completed hope it will be displayed in the Woodspring Museum, Burlington Street, Weston-super-Mare.

Locomotive No. 4 hauling the ex-Metropolitan coaches Nos. 8 and 16, seen here at Clevedon, with a train to Portishead, 25th June, 1938.　　*H.C. Casserley*

Appendix One

Weston, Clevedon & Portishead Tramway
Annual Returns 1898/9

The Board of Trade Annual Returns relating to Tramways made reference to the WC&P on two occasions only after the line had been opened to the public, for, in 1899, the Tramway became a Light Railway, and all subsequent returns were made under the heading of Railways.

Unlike the Railway Returns, which were made up to the 31st December of each year, the Tramway Returns were made up to the 30th June.

In the Returns for the year ending the 30th June, 1898, the Capital Expenditure of the WC&PT Company totalled £84,033 and this was made up thus:

	£
On lines and works open for traffic, including lands, building etc.	58,123
On Locomotives	2080
On Cars	3048
Legal & Parliamentary	7311
Miscellaneous Expenses	13,471

The Revenue Account showed a total expenditure of £1146 which was composed of:

	£
Maintenance of Way and Works	92
Locomotive Power	475
Traffic Expenses	430
Direction & Management	76
Any other working expenses	75

The Gross receipts from passengers totalled £1695 giving a net income of £549.

The following year, the total Capital Expenditure stood at £82,383 made up as follows:

	£
On lines and works open for traffic	52,975
On Locomotives	2275
On Cars	3682
Legal & Parliamentary	8445
Miscellaneous	15,006

Revenue account expenditure totalled £3362 which was formed by the following items:

	£
Maintenance of way & works	532
Locomotive Power	1045
Animal Power	575
Traffic Expenses	805*
Direction and Management	66
Rent of Offices, Stables & Sheds	78
Rates, Taxes and Tolls	15
Legal & Parliamentary	36
Any other expenses	210

* Including repairs and renewal of cars.

Receipts from passengers totalled £4198 — made up of £4055 from passengers, £70 from parcels and minerals, and £75 from other sources — giving a net income of £336.

Train Mileage

Year	Pass. Train Miles (Steam)	Pass. Train Miles (Rail Mtr)	Mixed Train Miles	Goods Train Miles	Shunting (Pass.) Miles	Shunting (Goods) Miles	Total Engine Miles*
1899			47,023	284			47,307
1900	No return made.						
1901	43,923		1660				45,583
1902	36,203			1177			37,380
1903	41,975			2468			44,443
1904	45,650			1642			47,292
1905	40,971		3547	387			44,905
1906	45,500		2763				48,263
1907	60,271		959				61,230
1908	75,562			7291			82,853
1909	61,655			7883			69,538
1910	56,976			7433			64,409
1911			61,378				61,378
1912			55,458				55,458
1913	29,995			29,995	420	420	60,830
1914–18	No Returns made during War.						
1919	16,950			16,950	254	254	34,408
1920	22,623			22,623	320	320	45,886
1921	20,091			20,091	2117	2118	44,417
1922	20,331	7612		20,331	1857	1858	51,989
1923	21,174	12,476		21,174	2138	2141	59,103
1924	17,006	19,264		17,006	2276	2274	57,826
1925	15,059	27,392		15,059	2406	2404	62,320
1926	13,675	19,294		13,514	1935	1930	50,348
1927	13,192	28,288		13,032	2518	2322	59,152
1928	12,972	30,506		12,972	2182	2183	60,815
1929	15,393	25,200		15,393	2055	2055	60,096
1930	13,479	28,960		13,463	2128	2132	60,162
1931	13,618	28,276		13,618	2124	2121	59,757
1932	13,400	28,932		13,368	2216	2219	60,135
1933	13,300	28,548		13,252	1942	1943	58,985
1934	13,714	28,820		13,562	1971	1969	60,036
1935	10,661	35,384		10,661	1671	1669	59,946
1936	10,136	35,640		10,136	1594	1595	59,101
1937	9403	36,010		9403	1533	1535	57,884
1938	9528	31,991		9464	1437	1437	53,857
1939–40	No Returns made for small railways in these years.						

*Mileages to 1912 inclusive were *train* mileages; thereafter, they were *engine* mileages.

Appendix Three

Number of Passengers Carried

Year	First class	Second class	Third/Parl.	Total	Season Tickets
1899	4246	234,456	3585	242,287	13
1900	No Return made.				
1901	5361	164,366	12,087	181,814	10
1902	4987	157,058	7582	169,627	9
1903	4460	155,253	8126	167,839	9
1904	4003	162,359	7086	173,448	5
1905	3314	145,737	5458	154,509	6
1906	2951	157,250	5613	165,814	10
1907	3479	183,518	6455	193,452	7
1908	3473	205,384	11,875	220,732	8
1909	2728	192,396	7911	203,035	13
1910	2662	186,163	7213	196,038	9
1911	2608	178,119		180,727	10
1912	1824	156,368	9442	167,634	10
1913	2105	181,666	5527	183,771	9
1914–18	No Returns during War.				
1919	1213	105,494	4497	106,707	24*
1920	916	111,838	8441	112,754	56
1921	309	77,679	11,621	77,988	41
1922	157	71,952	11,491	72,110	47
1923	150	97,137	12,334	97,287	30
1924	92	97,313	6184	97,405	16
1925	66	97,550	4903	97,616	14
1926	24	82,389	4817	82,413	13
1927	38	86,447	5186	86,485	14
1928	45	97,376	5684	97,421	9
1929	40	108,057	7321	108,097	11
1930	27	109,789	7435	109,816	18
1931	7	99,025	9367	99,030	8
1932	28	96,180	8162	96,208	6
1933	19	100,560	6674	100,579	5
1934	9	95,444	5405	95,453	4
1935	8	94,704	3589	94,712	4
1936	5	93,305	3730	93,310	4
1937	6	93,963	4532	93,969	7
1938	4	86,440	4266	86,444	6

1939–40 No Returns made for small railways in these years.

Workmen were classed as Third class passengers for the purpose of these Returns. As from 1913, workmen were calculated on a single journey basis and ceased to be counted in the gross totals.

In 1919, the individual totals included 1 First class and 7 Second class passengers free by Government Warrant, but these were not included in the gross totals.

* Season tickets calculated as the equivalent in annual tickets from this date.

Track Maintenance, details of material

Year	Ballast cu. yds	Fencing chs	Sleepers no.	Rails tons
1922	140	80	1000	
1923	200	20	945	
1924	200	20	574	
1925	190	20	751	
1926	300	20	1026	13
1927	150	40	878	
1928	50		699	
1929	50		723	
1930	75		435	
1931	100		421	
1932	150		452	
1933	200		667	
1934	150		804	
1935	120		1020	
1936	200		813	
1937	150		788	
1938	100		1187	

Kingston Road crossing c.1899 (viewed towards Clevedon). The gate on the left, with a white diamond, is being replaced by a cattle grid. The collection of notices are interesting, one being a 'Trespassers will be prosecuted' and the other two 'Beware of the trains'. *G. Rushton Collection*

A close up view of the treadle for operating traffic lights, March 1938. *L.G.R.P., courtesy David and Charles*

Appendix Five

Rolling Stock Repaired during the Year

Year	Locomotives			Carriages			Wagons			Railcars		
	a	b	c	a	b	c	a	b	c	a	b	c
1919	1	1	1	1		1		11	3			
1920	1	3	1		6	2		6	2			
1921	1	3	1		4	3		2	2			
1922	2	3	1	2	9	5	2	7	6			
1923	5	3	1	3	9	2	3	1	2			
1924	4	5	2	1	7		1	2	5			
1925	6	4	2	1*	11	1	2	8	2	1		
1926	4	7	3		9	2	4	4	2		3	
1927	3	2	1	2	7	3	3	5	1		1	
1928	2	3	1	1	5	2	3	4	2	1		
1929	2	3	2	1	7	4	2	8	5	1		
1930	1	2	1	2	3	2	2	4	4		2	
1931	2	2	1	2	5	2		6	4	1	1	
1932	1	1	1	2	1*		2	2	5		1	
1933	1	3	1	1	3*	2	2	3	4	1	1	
1934	2	2	2	2	2	3	2	3	5	1		
1935	3	2	2	2	3	3	2	3	5	1		
1936	1	3	1	1	3	3		4	6	1		
1937												
1938	1	1	2	2		2	4		6	2		

Column   a — Heavy Repairs
           b — Light Repairs
           c — Vehicles awaiting or undergoing repairs at the end of the Year
           * — Plus one other coaching vehicle

Note: Vehicles were counted each time they were repaired, so that the figure for 1925 — 6 locomotives — would mean that some engines were in for repair more than once.

Ex-MR brake van on the dump road, Clevedon, June 1937.
L.G.R.P., courtesy David and Charles

Appendix Six

Accounts 1897–1940

Accounts 1897–1909

Year	Number of Passengers carried	Receipts	Expenses	Profit or Loss
1 Dec. 1897–30th June, 1898	84,500	£1695	c£ 800	c+£ 895
1898 (July–Dec.)	138,000	£2682	£1601	+£1081
1899 (July–Dec.)	c122,000	£2413	£1641	+£ 772
1909	200,000(+)	£4000(−)	c£5000	−£1000(+)

Receiver's Accounts, 1910–1940

Year	Profit/Loss	Year	Profit/Loss
1910	+£ 253	1926	+£ 328
1911	+£ 229	1927	+£1687
1912	+£ 143	1928	−£ 651
1913	+£ 133	1929	+£ 322
1914	−£ 319	1930	+£ 803
1915	−£ 363	1931	+£ 43
1916	−£ 268	1932	−£ 318
1917	+£1419	1933	No figures available
1918–June 1921	−£ 908		
July 1921–June 1923	+£3970	1934	
July 1923–June 1924	−£ 480	1935	see
July 1924–Dec. 1924	+£ 296	1936	Appendix
1925	−£1386	1937	Seven
		1938	
		1939	
		1940 (to 18th May)	−£2452

Note: The increased profit in 1917 may have resulted from a severe curtailment of services and therefore of running-costs; that for 1921–3 coincides with the introduction of the first petrol railcar.

Wagon No. 19 (3 plank open, 7 ft wheelbase ex-Midland Railway) was used as a milk trailer running behind the small railcar, before the special wagon was purchased. Stanchions rested on the milk platform and prevented the side dropping right down. At Clevedon, 1938. *H.C. Casserley*

Appendix Seven

Detailed Accounts 1934–9

	1934			1935			1936		
Railway Receipts	£	s	d	£	s	d	£	s	d
Passengers	750	18	1	695	8	2	667	10	9
Season Tickets	8	15	4	4	7	8	6	14	10
Parcels etc.	57	2	6	41	5	6	37	8	4
Goods	83	7	0	192	8	2	187	19	7
Coal	248	8	3	241	10	1	260	3	11
Other Minerals	3050	3	4	2432	11	0	1168	2	11
Miscellaneous	24	5	5	15	12	3	7	11	8
	4222	**19**	**11**	**3623**	**2**	**10**	**2335**	**12**	**0**
Expenditure									
Maintenance of Way	687	7	2	686	16	3	537	15	5
Locomotive Repairs	276	0	4	161	18	8	171	10	10
Carriage Repairs	69	13	10	76	15	2	65	0	4
Wagon Repairs	31	17	4	30	2	6	27	1	1
Traffic Expenses	952	13	2	952	2	2	848	3	10
Loco. Running Expenses	831	18	6	752	7	10	825	6	4
General Charges	243	1	6	222	11	3	229	9	6
Compensation	70	13	2	74	14	6	72	10	5
Law Charges	5	0	0	5	0	0	11	6	0
Rates & Taxes (including Rate relief)	31	3	1	31	0	1	33	2	0
National Insurance	55	5	10	54	14	5	56	13	7
Mileage, Demurrage etc.	2	9	6	2	9	6	2	9	6
	3257	**3**	**5**	**3050**	**12**	**4**	**2880**	**8**	**10**
Net Railway Receipts	**965**	**16**	**6**	**572**	**10**	**6**	Dt **544**	**16**	**10**
Add:									
Miscellaneous Receipts —									
Rents from Houses & Lands	29	2	9	32	15	9	27	8	9
Other Rents	45	12	8	46	3	1	46	2	11
General Interest	Dt 72	16	5	Dt 71	5	5	Dt 72	15	11
	1	19	0	7	13	5		15	9
	967	**15**	**6**	**580**	**3**	**11**	Dt **544**	**1**	**1**
Deduct:									
Miscellaneous Charges —									
Chief Rents, Wayleaves etc.	**33**	**16**	**9**	**37**	**6**	**9**	**37**	**6**	**9**
	PROFIT:			**PROFIT:**			**LOSS:**		
Net Revenue	**933**	**18**	**9**	**542**	**17**	**2**	**581**	**7**	**10**

	1937			1938			1939		
Railway Receipts	£	s	d	£	s	d	£	s	d
Passengers	674	16	5	653	18	4	641	17	8
Season Tickets	13	2	8	12	14	9	12	13	3
Parcels etc.	38	18	5	39	15	9	33	9	5
Goods	286	6	4	203	4	9	387	7	1
Coal	270	0	8	283	0	1	324	16	5
Other Minerals	1320	6	9	1122	3	4	789	11	7
Miscellaneous	11	4	11	18	5	7	9	16	10
	2612	**16**	**2**	**2333**	**2**	**7**	**2199**	**12**	**3**
Expenditure									
Maintenance of Way	603	7	1	593	17	7	507	19	8
Locomotive Repairs	638	0	2	178	2	2	132	8	7
Carriage Repairs	82	2	7	35	11	6	48	17	11
Wagon Repairs	27	19	7	23	10	5	18	9	2
Traffic Expenses	835	18	8	728	14	3	642	3	2
Loco. Running Expenses	1013	14	2	911	15	2	847	7	11
General Charges	211	7	2	224	0	0	215	16	1
Compensation	65	4	2	72	5	2	67	12	10
Law Charges	11	6	0	8	3	0			
Rates & Taxes (including Rate relief)	31	1	4	34	19	10	37	13	7
National Insurance	53	13	5	47	11	9	43	5	11
Mileage, Demurrage etc.	2	9	6	2	9	6	2	9	6
	3576	**3**	**10**	**2860**	**18**	**4**	**2564**	**4**	**4**
Net Railway Receipts	Dt **963**	**7**	**8**	Dt **527**	**15**	**9**	Dt **364**	**12**	**1**
Add:									
Miscellaneous Receipts —									
Rents from Houses & Lands	32	18	3	27	16	3	36	16	1
Other Rents	47	12	4	53	14	8	58	18	6
General Interest	Dt 74	10	11	Dt 78	0	2	Dt 78	4	4
	5	**19**	**8**	**3**	**10**	**9**	**17**	**10**	**3**
	Dt **957**	**8**	**0**	Dt **524**	**5**	**0**	Dt **347**	**1**	**10**
Deduct:									
Miscellaneous Charges —									
Chief Rents, Wayleaves etc.	**37**	**6**	**9**	**37**	**6**	**9**	**37**	**6**	**9**
	LOSS:			LOSS:			LOSS:		
Net Revenue	**994**	**14**	**9**	**561**	**11**	**9**	**384**	**8**	**7**

Appendix Eight

Mineral Tonnage Carried

Date	Total minerals carried (excluding coal)
1st Jan., 1933– 6th Oct., 1933	76,481
1st Jan., 1934– 6th Oct., 1934	91,055
1st Jan., 1937–31st Dec., 1937	41,181
1st Jan., 1938–31st Dec., 1938	37,380
1st Jan., 1939–20th May, 1939	7 904

Tonnage Carried from Black Rock and Conygar Quarries

Date	Black Rock (tons)	Conygar (tons)
1st Jan., 1937–31st Dec., 1937	34,755	3968
1st Jan., 1938–31st Dec., 1938	27,937	7940
1st Jan., 1939–20th May, 1939	5 757	1469

Appendix Nine

WCPLR Staff 1925

At Clevedon

General Manager: A. Grundy
Station Agents: S. Grundy and G. Grundy

Train Crew No. 1	*Train Crew No. 2*	*Railcar Crew*
Driver — C. Coles	Driver — A. Barnes	Driver — A. Halliday
Fireman — T. Hedger	Fireman — A. Sharpe	Conductor — A. Jenkins
Guard — J. Riddick	Guard — E. C. Carey	

Porter — C. Toomey
Crossing Keeper — E. Day
Fitter — A. Hill
Fitter's Mate — B. Woodland
Day Cleaner — S. Plumley
Night Cleaner — F. Read
Carpenter — A. Ralph
Permanent Way Staff — J. Cooper, A. Taylor, J. Diamond, J. Brooks, J. Vowles, S. Badman, F. Thomas

At Portishead:

Station Master — F. Beere
Porter — F. Warren
Permanent Way — J. Robbins

At Worle Town:

Station Mistress — Florence Radford
Permanent Way — G. Gooding, F. Denmead, O. Simonds

At Weston-super-Mare:

Station Master — R. Surtees

Total: 33

Bibliography

(The Minute Books and other company papers belonging to the Light Railway have been missing for years).

A Locomotive History of Railways of the Isle of Wight. D. L. Bradley.
Portishead. Brown & Loosley.
The Trains We Loved. C. H. Ellis.
Somerset Harbours. G. Farr.
St Philip's Marsh. D. J. Fleming.
Industrial Railways of South Western England. Industrial Railway Society.
Light Railway Handbook. R. W. Kidner.
Somerset Railways. R. Madge.
Biographical Dictionary of Railway Engineers. J. Marshall.
Weston-super-Mare Tramways. C. G. Maggs.
Locomotives of the Great Western Railway. RCTS.
Weston, Clevedon & Portishead Railway. C. Redwood.
Railway Junction Diagrams 1914. Railway Clearing House.
The Colonel Stephens' Railways. J. Scott-Morgan.
Regional History of the Railways of Great Britain, Vol. 1. D. St. J. Thomas.
Reflections on the Portishead Branch. M. Vincent.
Weston, Clevedon & Portishead Light Railway. M. Windeatt (Typescript in Clevedon Library).
Minor Railways of England & their Locomotives. G. Woodcock.

Clevedon Mercury; GWR Magazine p. 311 1940; *The Locomotive,* particularly 1929; *Railway Magazine,* especially p. 524 1901, p. 415 June 1938, p. 116 1944, p. 71 1973; Railway Ticket Society Magazine May 1972 p. 167; Stephenson Locomotive Society Journal Vol. 51, No. 601 p. 251; *Trains Illustrated* August 1956 p. 393; *Western Daily Press; Weston-super-Mare Gazette; Weston Mercury.*

The first rail tractor purchased in 1921, seen at Clevedon just after its arrival. This Muir-Hill tractor, capable of hauling 60 tons, was mainly used for shunting on the jetty at Wick St Lawrence..   *E.H. Hazell*

Acknowledgements

Especial thanks is due to Peter Strange for kindly checking the manuscript.

Automatic Telephone & Electric Co. Ltd
J. Bennett
R. J. Bird, London Transport Museum
British Electric Traction
H. Carey
Miss F. Chaplin
J. H. Court
R. T. Coxon
W. H. Cullen
R. Day
M. E. J. Deane
Drewry Car Co. Ltd
English Electric Co. Ltd
E. R. Frears
A. H. Harbor
W. Hembury
Hudswell Clarke & Co. Ltd
R. Jordan

Miss A. Kearney
D. Kelham
J. Merrifield
T. Morgan
Nailsea & District Model Railway Club
Reverend A. Newman
North British Locomotive Co. Ltd
G. Ottley
W. Potter
Renishaw Iron Co. Ltd
D. Robertson
G. P. Rye
D. J. Steggles
M. J. Tozer
D.G. Venn
A. Westcott

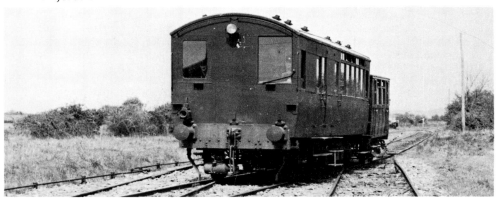

Railcar No. 5 and trailer passing Wick St Lawrence, June 1938.
L.G.R.P., courtesy David and Charles

The small railcar and trailer crossing Walton Road, c.1926. Note the trailer is not yet fitted with windows. *Author's Collection*

Index

f – 1 page following
ff – pages following